MUSEUM ECONOMICS AND THE COMMUNITY

New Research in Museum Studies: An International Series

Series Editor Dr Susan Pearce (Director, Department of Museum
Studies, University of Leicester)
Reviews Editor Dr Eilean Hooper-Greenhill

This important new series is designed to act as a forum for the
dissemination and discussion of new research currently being
undertaken in the field of museum studies. It covers the whole
museum field and, broadly, addresses the history and operation of
the museum as a cultural phenomenon. The papers are of
a high academic standard, but they are also intended to relate directly
to matters of immediate museum concern. The series fills a
major gap in the present scope of museum-based literature.

NEW RESEARCH IN MUSEUM STUDIES
An International Series

2

Museum Economics and the Community

Edited by Susan Pearce

THE ATHLONE PRESS
London & Atlantic Highlands, NJ

First published 1991 by The Athlone Press Ltd
1 Park Drive, London NW11 7SG and
171 First Avenue, Atlantic Highlands, NJ 07716

© The Athlone Press 1991

British Library Cataloguing in Publication Data
A catalogue record for
this title is available from
the British Library

ISBN 0 485 90002 5

Library of Congress Cataloging-in-Publication Data
Museum economics and the community/edited by Susan Pearce.
   p. cm. – (New research in museum studies: an international
series : 2)
   Includes bibliographical references and index.
   ISBN 0-485-90002-5
   1. Museums I. Pearce, Susan M. II. Series: New research
in museum studies : v. 2.
AM5.M923 1992
069.1 – dc20

Typeset by GCS, Leighton Buzzard, Bedfordshire
Printed in Great Britain by the University Press, Cambridge

Contents

Part Three
Reviews edited by *Eilean Hooper-Greenhill*

List of Figures

List of Tables

List of Plates

Editorial Introduction

SUSAN M. PEARCE

In Part One of its second volume *New Research in Museum Studies* turns to issues focusing on ways in which museums function as economic and social institutions within their communities. This is a very large and increasingly significant area, and the papers collected here look at a broad range of topics, as both befits the subject and follows the scope and style which *New Research in Museum Studies* established in Volume 1, *Objects of Knowledge*.

An important area of debate surrounds the ways in which museum operations should be managed and financed in a climate of scarce resources in which difficult choices have to be made. This area is explored by Peter Johnson and Barry Thomas, using as illustrative material their research into the impact of the North of England Open Air Museum at Beamish on the local economy. Close cousin to economic considerations are those surrounding value for money and quality of service. These involve an ability to measure the performance of museums, and bring us to the need for performance indicators, the conceptual, measurement and behavioural problems of which are discussed by Peter Jackson.

Economic considerations must try to match the needs and hopes of the community the museum serves; otherwise we shall see museums losing their hearts and souls in the struggle to become leaner and fitter, in a kind of moral anorexia, and operating in increasing detachment from the people around them. A particular theme is the rights and needs of the visually impaired and disabled, whose right to normality in the museum context is most eloquently expressed by Nick Pearson, who draws on his personal experiences. The balance between 'professional' needs and 'public' needs is further pursued by Guy Wilson with particular reference to the Royal Armouries. Patricia Kell draws a number of these issues together in her account of the 'living history' project at the Fortress of Louisbourg, Cape Breton Island, Canada.

In Part Two of this volume, *New Research in Museum Studies* has taken the opportunity to include two papers which depart from the topic of the volume, following the intention expressed in the *Call for Papers* in Volume 1, *Objects of Knowledge* (p. 229). The essay by William Chapman embraces an important study of Augustus Pitt Rivers and the idea of the typological museum, and that by Charles Hunt raises the issue of the relationship between words and things in an African context. Both papers were contributed as a result of debates raised in Volume 1. Part Three continues our practise of offering a wide range of reviews of museum-related media.

PART ONE

1

Museums: an economic perspective

PETER JOHNSON and BARRY THOMAS

Introduction

The purpose of this essay[1] is to look at museum operations from an economic perspective, and thereby to contribute to current debates on how such operations should be managed and financed and on appropriate policies towards them. A central concern of economic analysis is the efficiency with which resources – land, labour, capital and management – are allocated to different uses. This concern derives from the scarcity of resources: resources that are allocated to museum activities cannot be utilized elsewhere in the economy or *vice versa*. Choices therefore have to be made. The same problem of scarcity also arises in the allocation of resources between museums and between functions and activities *within* museums.

The efficiency of resource allocation can only be assessed within the context of given policy objectives. It is not the task of economic analysis to say *which* objectives should be chosen; thus such analysis is relevant in the museum field whether the underlying objective is, for example, the maximization of the general welfare of the population, museum profits, Exchequer gains, visitor numbers or scholarly output. 'Economic' is not therefore synonymous with 'commercial' or 'profit-making'. Economic analysis may also show how different objectives may be achieved through various strategies, thereby offering the policymaker a 'menu' of objectives from which to choose. In this way, the analysis may sometimes have an important clarifying role. (Policy objectives are often very unclear or even non-existent.) In addition, it may provide some guidance on the trade-offs that may exist between policy objectives.

In this essay we focus on the efficiency with which resources are allocated to, and within, the museums sector. The first two sections provide the context for the discussion, briefly reviewing the scale, characteristics and financing of the UK museums sector, and examining the nature of museum 'output'. The key influences on resource allocation are costs and demand and these are discussed in two further sections. The case for public funding is examined in the following section and in the next the question of resource allocation is directly addressed. Pricing is clearly relevant for such allocation and is currently the subject of much debate. It is therefore considered separately in the penultimate section. The final section concludes the paper by suggesting some potentially fruitful avenues for future research.

Illustrative material in this paper draws on some research the authors are undertaking into the economic impact of the North of England Open Air Museum at Beamish on the local economy (Johnson and Thomas, 1990a and b). Beamish cannot in any sense be regarded as 'typical' of all UK museums, but it does face problems and challenges that are widespread among the latter.

The museums sector

A definition
In this paper it is not necessary to engage in an extended debate on a precise definition of 'museum'. The Museums Association's definition, used in its database project, is sufficient for our purposes: a museum is 'an institution which collects, documents, preserves, exhibits and interprets material evidence and associated information for the public benefit' (Museums Association, 1987a: 6). A museum is thus a kind of vertically integrated firm which transforms resources into output. From an economic perspective, the Museums Association's definition raises two questions of resource allocation. Firstly, how should resources be distributed across the various activities that are mentioned? And, secondly,, what is 'the public benefit' and who decides it? Both questions are considered at various points throughout this paper.

Museums in the UK: scale, characteristics and financing
Here we examine briefly the scale and key characteristics of museum activity in the UK, and the financing of such activity. We need first, however, to look at the underlying rationale for examining museums as a group.

The museums 'sector'   There are bound to be some institutions over which there is some doubt as to whether they should be labelled as museums. As a result it is inevitable that the museums 'sector' or 'industry' is rather imprecisely defined at the margin. Nevertheless from a resource allocation viewpoint, there is a good case for sometimes grouping museums together as an entity. They have much in common on the *supply* side: the 'technologies' and procedures – in (for example) classification and documentation – that they use are often broadly similar and they frequently compete in the same specialist labour market. On the *demand* side, the products offered by different museums are often seen, rightly or wrongly, as closely related. This relatedness of museum products means that a change in one museum's strategy on (for example) pricing, the quality of the visitor experience offered, or marketing is likely to have an impact on other museums. Similar relatedness may also exist in research and scholarship, with museums complementing and/or competing with other museums in these functions. It should be noted that interdependence may also exist between museums and quite different activities and institutions. For instance, some visitors may go to the north east because they wish jointly to 'consume' Beamish, the Metro Centre and Washington Wild Fowl Park: so improving the attractiveness of one may boost demand for the others. On the other hand, Beamish and such other attractions may be substitutes. The 1990 National Garden Festival at Gateshead, for example, may reduce visitor numbers to Beamish. Visiting Beamish may also be a substitute for leisure activities such as fishing or golf. For some museums, interrelationships may be closer with non-museum organizations than with some other museums. What is clear, however, is that resource allocation in a museum cannot be considered independently of such allocation in other related organizations.

The scale and characteristics of museum activity   The most comprehensive source of data on museums in the UK is the 1985 database developed by the Museums Association and the subsequent update of that exercise (Museums Association, 1987a and b). In October 1986 there were 2,131 museums employing over 10,000 full-time staff on the database. Of these, 1,587 (75 per cent) responded to the update questionnaire. Some basic information on the respondent museums is given in Table 1. (The focus in this table is on visitor numbers. Such numbers may not, however, always be an appropriate indicator of the scale of a museum's activities, particularly where a substantial research undertaking is involved.) The three categories of museums

given in Table 1 relate to individual institutions. These institutions
may be part of bigger organizations. For example, of the 120 national
and government department museums included in Table 1, 36 per
cent were branch museums (Museums Association, 1987b: 5). Table 1
must be treated cautiously because the 1,587 museums represent only
a proportion, albeit a very significant one, of the total number in the
UK. Furthermore, only 65 per cent of the respondent museums
provided data on visitor numbers. (Not surprisingly the response was
higher among central and local government museums.) Despite these
limitations, however, it seems evident from the table that 'public
sector' museums account for the majority (78 per cent) of visitors.

National and government departments account for less than one
tenth of the number of museums but nearly four tenths of visitors.
They are also highly concentrated: the UK's four largest national
museums and galleries (NMGs)[2] attracted 56 per cent of all visitors to
NMGs in 1988 (Museums and Galleries Commission, 1988: 40).
Large-scale operations are relatively more common in this category:
47 per cent of the national and government department museums for
whom visitor numbers are available had over 100,000 visitors in

Table 1   *UK museums: numbers and visitors, 1985/6*

1	2	3	4	5
Type	Number of respondent museums	% of total number of respondent museums	Visitors (m)	Visitors as % of total number of visitors to respondent museums
National and government department	120	8	28	38
Local authority	537	34	29	40
Other	930	58	16	22
TOTAL	1,587	100	73	100

Source: Museums Association, 1987b.

1985/6, whereas corresponding figures for local authority and 'other' museums were 10 and 8 per cent respectively.

The national and government department museums have a much stronger commitment to scholarship and research than do other categories. This is reflected in their staffing figures: they have over 50 per cent of UK museum staff, compared with 38 per cent of visitors.

Trends in visitor numbers are difficult to establish because of the absence of consistent time series data. However, the limited data presented in Table 2 suggests that the second half of the 1980s has seen a major growth in museum visiting, although this has not been shared by the nationals. The Museums Association study (Museums Association, 1987b: 7) suggests that the main growth in visitor numbers has been in the local authority museums (up by over 25 per cent between 1984 and 1985 alone). Visitor numbers have clearly been

Table 2   *Visitor trends in museums, GB (000s)*

	National museums	All museums[a]
1978	25,661	
1979	26,011	
1980	25,483	
1981	23,283	
1982	22,669	
1983	23,793	
1984	24,541	
1985	25,562	68,000
1986	25,447	73,000
1987	25,263	80,000
1988	24,886[b]	
1989		100,000

Sources: HMSO, 1989c and Museums and Galleries Commission, 1988).
Notes:
[a]To the nearest million. These figures are derived from HMSO (1989c): 5. The 1985 and 1986 figures appear to come from the Museums Association databank figures for 1984/5 and 1985/6 respectively. If so, they would more appropriately be assigned to 1984 and 1985. These figures do in any case only relate to visitors to a sample, albeit a substantial one, of museums and are therefore underestimates. It is not clear whether the figures given for 1987 and 1989 are consistent with those for the earlier years. It is assumed that they are.
[b]Estimated from *Sightseeing 1988*.

Table 3 *Sources of income by type of museum*

Type of income	All museums	National museums	Government department museums	Local authority museums	Other museums
			% of Total Income		
Revenue grants[a]	68	75	65	80	41
Special project grants[b]	8	14	9	2	2
Earned income[c]	16	10	26	16	31
Grants and allocations[d]	3	1	–	1	8
Supplementary income[e]	5	–	–	–	18
TOTAL	100	100	100	100	100

Source: Museums Association, 1987a: 153.

Notes:

[a] Revenue grants and allocations from public sources.

[b] Grants and allocations from public bodies for specific functions (including acquisitions) from central and local government and national museums.

[c] Earned income, through sales, admission charges, professional service fees, rentings, lettings and business sponsorship.

[d] Grants and allocations from private sources (including the National Arts Collections Fund, covenanted monetary gifts from Corporations and individuals, the Beecroft Bequest).

[e] Supplementary income (interest received, dividends, sale of securities, income generated by friends organizations, income from charitable trusts, trading companies, net receipts from fund-raising, and net income from income-generating projects and other activities).

A dash represents less than one per cent.

Table 4   *Distribution of different categories of income across museum types*

Type of income	All museums	National museums	Government department museums	Local authority museums	Other museums
Revenue grants	100	58	–	30	12
Special project grants	100	84	3	7	6
Earned income	100	27	4	24	46
Grants and allocations	100	8	–	12	80
Supplementary income	100	2	–	17⁻	91

Source: Museums Association, 1987a: 153.
Note: The definitions of the income types are those given in Table 3 (p. 10). A dash indicates less than one per cent.
one per cent.

growing faster than national income, an indication that museum visiting is perceived as a luxury good.

Important developments in the nature and type of museums in recent years are not captured by the visitor figures. For example, nearly half of the institutions covered by the Museums Association survey were formed after 1971 (three quarters since the Second World War). Furthermore, of the museums founded since 1950, well over half have been in the non-public sector, with the majority of these being set up by voluntary associations or individuals. The most recent study of the independent museums (Policy Studies Institute, 1989: 17) reports strong growth in this sector in the 1970s and 1980s.

Financing A breakdown of sources of income for different museum categories is given in Tables 3 and 4. (National and government department museums are separated in these tables.) These figures are now becoming a little dated but they are still the most comprehensive available. They must be treated carefully, since there may be some response bias: only 44 per cent of museums responded with suitable data and it may well be that the non-respondents tend to be those with a particular structure of income (e.g. more dependence on private sources).

Table 3 shows the dominance of public sources of finance for the publicly-owned museums. Even in the 'private sector' museums (the last column) revenue grants account for over 40 per cent of their income. Not surprisingly, it is museums in this sector which rely to the greatest relative extent on earned and supplementary income. Less than a quarter of these museums allowed free admission in 1985/6 compared with over half of the national and government department museums and over 60 per cent of local authority museums (Museums Association, 1987b: 16). From Table 4, it is evident that the nationals have by far the biggest share of all revenue and special project grants going to the museums sector as a whole, whereas their shares of grants and allocations and supplementary income are all relatively low. If the data in Tables 1 and 4 are combined it is clear that the average revenue subsidy for the visitor to a national museum is very much higher than that for a visitor to a museum in the other categories.

A comprehensive, detailed picture of trends in public expenditure on museums is difficult to obtain. One reason for this difficulty is that in recent years there has been a number of transfers of responsibility between agencies. The abolition of the Greater London Council and the Metropolitan Counties in 1986 led to central government funding of museums previously in the local government sector. In the late 1980s, responsibility for the buildings of the national museums was transferred from the Property Services Agency to the museums themselves. The funding of the Natural History Museum was also transferred from the Department of Education and Science to the Office of Arts and Libraries. And in 1988/89, running costs for many national museums included for the first time substantial sums for pension contributions not previously shown on museum votes (Museums and Galleries Commission, 1988: 10). These changes mean that time series data on expenditure by type of museum and/or funding agency frequently vary across studies, since analysts often use different methods to ensure consistency over time: compare, for example, the expenditure data in HMSO (1989a) and Policy Studies Institute (1989). The most comprehensive recent analysis, however, is contained in the latter. Table 5 uses this source to provide summary data on UK public expenditure (1984/85 prices) on museums and galleries. The real increase between 1984/85 and 1988/89 for central government in England, Wales and Northern Ireland, and local government in England – together accounting for over 87 per cent of all public expenditure in 1987/88 – was 14.3 per cent. This compares with a real increase in gross domestic product over the same period of 16.6 per cent.[3] Visitor numbers have almost certainly grown faster than public expenditure (see Table 2, p. 9); thus the average subsidy each visitor receives has gone down.

In recent years the funding of the NMGs has attracted considerable debate. The Museums and Galleries Commission has presented evidence (1988: 10) to show that the increases in grants towards running costs in the 1980s has not been enough to match increased responsibilities of the NMGs or the increases in salaries of museum staff. Government expenditure plans published in June 1989 (HMSO, 1989a) show that the planned increase in *running* costs for 1989/90–1990/91 for all the English NMGs except the National Gallery was well below the rate of inflation. The seriousness of the position was emphasized in 1988 by the Commission which concluded:

> This funding gap is serious, and has had adverse consequences in all the national museums, which have had to leave unfilled varying numbers of posts in their complements (though these were determined after Government staff inspections). The effects are lamentably to be seen in terms of closed galleries, reduced security, curtailed opening hours or days . . . ,

Table 5 *Public expenditure on museums and galleries (1984/5 prices)*

	1984/5	1985/6	1986/7	1987/8	1988/9
Central Government					
England	101.7	104.4	113.9	115.3	131.2
Scotland	9.4	9.0	10.4	12.9	n.a.
Wales	6.9	7.4	7.3	8.2	9.8
Northern Ireland	3.9	4.1	4.4	4.5	4.6
TOTAL CENTRAL GOVERNMENT	122.0	124.8	135.9	140.8	n.a.
Local Government					
England	82.9	85.0	74.7	77.7	77.7[a]
Scotland	n.a.	n.a.	12.3[b]	12.4[b]	n.a.
Wales	2.5	2.7	2.8	3.7	n.a.
Northern Ireland	n.a.	0.5	0.5[b]	0.5[b]	n.a.
TOTAL LOCAL GOVERNMENT	n.a.	n.a.	90.5	94.8	n.a.

Source: Policy Studies Institute, 1989: 4.

Notes:

[a] The Policy Studies Institute (PSI) study (1989: 4) on which this table is based does not provide a figure for local government expenditure in 1988/89. However, Office of Arts and Libraries data (HMSO, 1989c: 42) suggests that there was no change in real terms between 1987/8 and 1988/9. The PSI figure for 1987/8 was therefore used.

[b] The PSI study only provides these data in current prices. The same deflator applied to the other parts of the UK has therefore been used to arrive at the constant prices figure given in the table.

backlogs of work (e.g. on conservation and the production of catalogues and other scholarly publications), less ability to help schools..., inefficient use of staff time (wordprocessors can hardly be afforded), and less good service to the public.... Most serious is the danger of a cumulative, long-term decline in curatorial standards, as reduced staff are increasingly stretched and often unable to maintain contact with other international scholars, find time to attend international gatherings, take necessary study leave or publish accumulated experience (Museums and Galleries Commission, 1988: 12).

In the absence of compensating growth in other sources of income and/or increases in internal efficiency, such adverse effects are an inevitable consequence of the squeeze on funds, which in turn is a result of reductions in the overall scale of public expenditure and on the rankings given to competing claims on that expenditure. If as a result of the change in the size and/or distribution of the public expenditure, the allocation going to museums is reduced, adjustment problems are to be expected.

There are two other aspects of current financial policy towards national museum finances that should be noted. First, the government is keeping constant in cash terms the purchase grants available to the museums, on the grounds that higher priority should be given 'to the care and management of the existing collections, with emphasis on conservation, storage and upkeep of the buildings in which they are housed' (HMSO, 1989c: 45). Second, the government is explicitly committed to a 'plural' funding system in which museums are encouraged to develop other sources of funds, notably through admission charges but also through the commercial exploitation of their physical and human assets. The museums along with the rest of the arts are to be encouraged to be more 'self-reliant' in development and growth (HMSO, 1989b: 2). However, the government has endeavoured to ensure that responsibility for introducing admission charges in the NMGs is not attributed to this policy: its 'official' stance towards such charges is one of neutrality, and it has placed sole responsibility for this issue on Boards of Trustees (HMSO, 1989b: vi).

Some implications for resource allocation   The figures given in this section show that the NMGs rely very heavily on public funding, and take a share of the latter which is far higher than their share of visitors. Furthermore, the number of visitors going to NMGs as a whole is fairly static. These characteristics raise important questions of resource allocation. Why should the NMGs continue to have such a high proportion of public funds when their visitor numbers have not been growing? What is the underlying rationale for their public funding anyway? The latter question could also be asked of local authority sponsored museums. Part of the answer may lie in the nature of museum output and it is to the definition of that output that we now turn.

Museum output

Resources are used in order to produce output; any discussion of resource allocation therefore requires the latter to be defined.

Intermediate versus final output

Output in a museum may be 'intermediate' (in which case it becomes an input into another productive process) or 'final'. The provision of collections and documentation which serve as a resource base for researchers may be regarded as intermediate output. The service of running a repository for the nation's treasures is also a form of intermediate output: there is little point in such activity unless, *at some future time*, these treasures are used as a basis for research and/or exhibitions.

Final output is usually of two main types. The first is the fruits of scholarship (which for our purposes includes research). This is expressed through publications, lectures and in the development of exhibitions. The national museums have, of course, been very active in producing such output and often have worldwide reputations as a result (see, for example, Museums and Galleries Commission, 1988: 6). Major consumers of scholarly output are other scholars. The second type of final output is the 'experience' enjoyed by the general public when they make a visit. The balance between intermediate and final output raises important questions over the advantages and disadvantages of different levels of vertical integration: there is no *technical* reason why the function of providing a resource base for scholars and of scholarship itself should be integrated, although for a number of reasons it may make sense.

The distribution of resources across the production of the two types of final output varies between museums. As indicated above, the NMGs are strongly committed to scholarly activities. Indeed they have become 'the intellectual hub around which all the nation's museum system must revolve if it is to command the respect and affection of its paymasters, who are in the end its visiting public' (Museum and Galleries Commission, 1986: 103). They are, however, also required to promote public understanding and enjoyment. Most other museums focus on the latter kind of output and often have insufficient resources to devote to extensive scholarly activity.

All museum displays rely to a greater or lesser extent on scholarly output; indeed they may sometimes be the principal channel of such output. (In this sense scholarly output may also be seen as an intermediate output, feeding into the visitor experience.) Although scholarly output and the visitor experience may be closely related in this way, it is helpful for expositional purposes to give them separate treatment.

Final output

Scholarly output   Output of this kind has some important economic characteristics. It has elements of a 'public good' in the sense that there is 'non-rivalry' in consumption – one person's consumption of research findings might not impede another's consumption of those same findings – and 'non-excludability'. The latter characteristic is a direct consequence of the fact that research results are likely to be in the public domain. Thus no one can be excluded from consuming them once they are produced. (Indeed, a good case can be made for arguing that published results *should* be freely available, since the absorption of such results by other scholars imposes no further production costs.) As a result of these two public good characteristics the scholarly output of museums is, as we shall see, unlikely to be supplied to the optimal extent through a private market system and public support may therefore be necessary.

The visitor experience   This experience results from the combination of the museum's provision of services and the visitor's participation. In this sense the latter is part of the productive process (Peacock and Godfrey, 1974). It should be noted that the visitor experience is affected, perhaps crucially, not only by exhibits and the interpretation provided but also by a whole range of 'non-museum' services such as toilet facilities, catering and retailing. The experience is not limited to the time spent at the museum: anticipation and subsequent memories of a visit may extend the period over which the experience is enjoyed. It may sometimes be possible to enjoy some of the experience without physically making a visit (through videos and publications).

The *number* of visitors will often be an important influence on the average visitor experience. This influence may be felt in several ways. First, numbers may affect the general atmosphere at the museum: too few visitors may leave each visitor feeling isolated; too many may generate cramped conditions. Second, the level of queuing, e.g. to exhibits, car parks and other facilities, is positively related to the number of visitors. Third, where capacity constraints differ across different sections of the museum, visitor numbers will influence which mix of exhibits can be visited at peak times. Table 6 provides a crude indication of capacity limits at different locations on the Beamish site. The estimates, which are illustrative only, must be treated very cautiously because of the assumptions involved. Despite these limitations, it is clear from column 4 of the table – which expresses capacity as a percentage of the average daily number of visitors in August 1989 – that the proportion of visitors who can enjoy an exhibit or facility varies significantly between points in the museum, and that a visitor in that month will have an experience which is rather different from that of a visitor in, say, May where the average daily number of visitors is almost half that of the August figure.

The nature of the visitor experience and its determinants are vitally important for management planning. They are highly relevant to the analysis of demand and of forecasting since *ceteris paribus*, a poor visitor experience is likely to depress demand. A clear view of what kind of experience should be on offer is also relevant for investment decisions. If, for example, it is thought that an essential feature of the experience should be the viewing of a particular exhibit, there is little point in investing in parts of the museum which have capacity limits greater than that exhibit.

Spillover Scholarly output may generate spillover benefits or 'positive externalities', that is, benefits which do not accrue to the purchaser of scholarly output. For instance, one individual's 'consumption' of a publication may have an educative effect on others. Again, someone who has made a visit to a museum may generate greater knowledge and appreciation of the past in others. In the case of Beamish, the availability of the 'Beamish experience' has stimulated a greater sense of regional identity, awareness and pride in the area's industrial heritage. These spillover effects may be very widespread. As Robbins has argued:

Table 6 *Beamish Museum: some illustrative estimates of capacity*

1 Facility	2 Assumptions on which estimates of maximum daily physical capacity of facility are based	3 Estimated maximum daily physical capacity of facility	4 Column 3 as percentage of 3,590 (the average daily attendance in August, 1989)
Midday meal in tearoom	30 minutes per meal; 3.5 people per table; 45 tables; meals served 12.00–2.0 p.m.	630 midday meals	17.5
Morning coffee/ afternoon tea	15 minutes per refreshment; 3.5 people per table; 45 tables; coffee/tea served for 2 hours	1,260 morning coffees/ afternoon teas	35.1
Drift mine	3 groups of 12 people; 10 minutes per visit; 7 hours 'effective' opening	2,520	70.2

Train/bus	3 trains/buses with 200 passengers; 13 minute journey including turnaround; empty from town to entrance: 10.00 a.m.–2.00 p.m. Empty from entrance to town: 2.00 p.m.–6.00 p.m.	3,692	102.8
A colliery cottage	Estimated by management	2,500	69.6
The four colliery cottages	Estimated by management	10,000	278.6
A shop in the town	Estimated by management	5,000	139.3
The three shops in the town	Estimated by management	15,000	417.8
The dentist's house in the town	Estimated by management	2,400	66.9
The town as a whole	Estimated by management; the number above which the 'overall' experience of the town deteriorates	3,500	97.5
Car park	2,100 car spaces; 3.5 passengers in each car; 40 coaches, each with 45 visitors; each space used once per day	9,150	254.9

the positive effects of the fostering of art and learning and the
preservation of culture are not restricted to those immediately prepared to
pay cash but diffuse themselves to the benefit of much wider sections of
the community in much the same way as the benefits of the apparatus of
public hygiene or of a well-planned landscape (1963: 58).

There may also be wider economic benefits: a museum may attract
visitors who in turn generate a wide range of spin-off benefits in the
economy. (For a recent analysis of such benefits from Beamish, see
Johnson and Thomas, 1990b. Myerscough (1988) includes an
examination of the economic impact of museums within that for the
arts as a whole at a national level.) For example, incoming visitors
may generate demand for leisure facilities that the local community
can also enjoy and which would not otherwise exist.

As we shall see in subsequent sections the existence of spillover
effects may have important implications for public funding and
resource allocation.

Output for whom?   Scholarly output produced in this generation
remains available for subsequent generations. The same may not be
true for visitor experiences: there may be a trade-off between
providing an experience for the current generation's visitors and
serving those from subsequent generations. In extreme cases, certain
exhibits if viewed or handled by the current generation may become
worn out. For example, Beamish faces a finite supply of old buses and
trams. If these are used to transport passengers within the museum,
they will eventually cease to exist. Thus preservation of such exhibits
for future generations to experience may entail restrictions on the
experiences of the present generation (unless, of course, replicas are
acceptable). Another type of trade-off may occur where resources are
put into collection activities in order to preserve the option for future
generations to view their past. At the time that items for collection
become available, museum staff may not know whether there is likely
to be any demand in the future to view such objects. However if they
are not collected they may be lost for ever. This possibility dominated
the early catholic collecting policy of Frank Atkinson, Beamish
Museum's first director: 'It is essential that collecting be carried out
as quickly and on as a big a scale as possible. It is now *almost* too late;
buildings, farm implements, domestic utensils are being scrapped
every day. Customs, traditions are all dying out'.[4] More resources put
into collections (and consequent cataloguing and preservation) will
usually mean less for servicing current generation visitors.

Trade-offs of the above kind are obviously of importance for resource allocation. We shall return to these issues later in the paper.

Costs

The importance of accurate cost data

Any examination of the allocation of resources requires an accurate picture of the costs that arise from utilizing those resources. The key concept of the economist is opportunity cost: the cost of using a resource is the best return it could obtain in some alternative use. How such costs should be measured is a matter of some debate. However, one widely used method takes the market price of the resource as a proxy. Although such an approach is not entirely satisfactory – market prices may be subject to distortions, e.g. from the exercise of monopoly power – it is often the best available. It must be remembered that for many museums in the public sector, costs reported in their accounts will not reflect the resources contributed by other organizations. For instance, much of the accounting work for Beamish is undertaken by Cleveland County Council; at Ironbridge, staff have been seconded by the local authority, and their salaries paid by the latter. We have also seen that until recently, most of the NMGs did not pay for the maintenance of their buildings. Even where a museum makes a payment which is recorded in its accounts that payment may not reflect the true opportunity cost of the resource involved. At Beamish, the rental charged for the site is substantially lower than the value of the land in alternative uses. Accurate estimates of costs faced by the museum will require adjustments to be made which reflect these subsidies.

Even where costs paid by the museum are accurately estimated, there may still be some wider costs which arise as the result of museum activities which do not have to be met by the museum itself. (These are negative externalities which are the conceptual counterparts to the positive externalities mentioned earlier.) For example, the cost of road congestion caused by high visitor demand does not have to be 'paid for' by the museum but by those who are affected by such congestion.

The structure of costs

The scholarly output produced by a museum is likely to be fairly closely related to the number of staff engaged in scholarly activity.

Output may rise more than proportionately as staff increase – because of the existence of synergic interaction between staff – but such advantages may not persist beyond fairly low staffing levels. Whether or not such economies of scale exist, it remains true that scholarly output cannot be increased without more staff (assuming that all staff are fully employed).

When it comes to visitor experience output the picture is rather different. For a given museum 'capacity' the core staff will not change as the number of visitors changes. Many other costs apart from core staff costs will also remain invariant with respect to visitor numbers. It is true that some labour costs may vary – for example temporary guides and additional security staff may be taken on at peak times – but these are likely to be relatively small. Some notion of the way in which costs vary with visitor numbers at Beamish can be obtained from Table 7 which is based on data collected in 1988. Only the weekly wage bill (inclusive of National Insurance and pensions) is considered. Nearly all monthly staff are appointed on a 'year round' basis and most other costs are similarly 'fixed'. The third column in the table gives an estimate of 'marginal' costs, i.e. the addition to total cost resulting from increasing visitor numbers by one. This table ignores some other costs such as electricity and maintenance for the trams and bus, which may be used more intensively as visitor numbers increase. Per visitor, however, these costs are relatively small. (It is important to note that these marginal cost estimates are derived from seasonal fluctuations; care must be taken when using them to indicate how costs might vary with visitor numbers *in any given time period*.)

The cost structure for the visitor experience – high fixed costs and

Table 7 *Estimates of marginal cost*

Months (1988)	1 Change in visitor numbers	2 Change in total weekly labour costs (£)	3 'Marginal' costs i.e. $\frac{2}{1}$ (£)
February–April	+40,491	+17,311	0.43
April–June	+26,997	+ 4,068	0.15
June–August	+38,441	+ 4,816	0.13

low and falling marginal costs – has some important implications for the operation of museums. It means that the opportunities for adjusting costs to visitor flows at least in the short run are restricted. In the longer term, of course, capacity and staffing can be adjusted. For example, buildings can be closed and sold off and natural wastage can enable a museum to reduce its staff. For the expanding museum, a buildings programme can be undertaken and new staff taken on.

The short run cost structure of museums such as Beamish which have pronounced seasonal fluctuations, means *inter alia* that any boostings of off-peak visitor demand will hardly affect costs, but will increase revenue. It also means that if visitors are charged marginal costs only – and there is a good theoretical case for this from an efficiency viewpoint (see p. 31–32) – a museum will not cover its *total* costs, and will have to obtain deficit funding. On the capital side, it is worth noting that a substantial proportion of the capital stock of UK museums is the result of past gifts and bequests (Peacock and Godfrey, 1974). While such generosity may alleviate the pressure on a museum's purchasing budget, it inevitably has implications for running costs, arising, for example, from restoration and preservation. In some cases, a gift is made on conditions that inhibit the receiving museum's subsequent freedom to alter the composition of its assets or the structure of its running costs. (For example, these conditions may restrict the sale of the asset and/or may impose particular preservation costs.)

Demand

In this section we examine, firstly, the demand for scholarly output and the visitor experience which is expressed by individuals in the market place, and, secondly, whether this demand is an adequate reflection of the total social demand for these outputs.

Market demand

Demand for scholarly output   There are a number of ways in which private individuals and institutions may directly express their 'demand' for the scholarly output of a museum. First, they may buy its publications. They may also purchase its research, advisory or consultancy services. Second, the museum may receive bequests and donations. Third, individuals and businesses may provide sponsorship for scholarly activities. Such sponsorship will often be given with an eye more to the publicity that is generated than to the research results that are made possible, i.e. the sponsor buys a type of output which is different from that whose production is being financed. (Here publicity and scholarly output are joint products.) Finally, there may be some 'derived' demand for scholarly output via the demand for the visitor experience (see below). It may be possible to influence these different expressions of demand for scholarship by promotional activities.

Demand for the visitor experience   It is in principle possible to construct a visitor demand schedule of the kind illustrated in Figure 1. This schedule, AV_2 in the diagram, shows the relationship between the admission price and visitor numbers, holding all other factors constant. The schedule relates to an appropriate time period and its position and shape are determined by a number of factors such as tastes, income and the availability and price of substitutes. For ease of exposition we have depicted it as linear. It is downward sloping to the right, because visitor numbers increase as the admission price falls. If admission were free, V_2 visitors would be attracted to the museum. It is important to stress that the demand schedule in Figure 1 is based on the assumption that the quality of the visitor experience

Figure 1   *Museum demand*

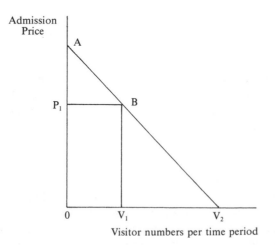

Visitor numbers per time period

is constant, i.e. it abstracts from the possibility that the number of visitors will influence the experience received. We shall return to Figure 1 later in the paper.

Relatively little formal work has been undertaken into the determinants of visitor demand for museums. However, Darnell *et al.* (1990) have recently undertaken some econometric modelling of visitor flows at Beamish. Their model 'explains' visitor numbers in each quarter in terms of the admission price, the price of all other goods and services, incomes, the weather and quality.[5] The results of this modelling exercise are instructive. First, it is clear that within the range of admission prices actually experienced at Beamish, demand is not very sensitive to the admission price. The price elasticity of demand – which may be defined as the proportionate change in the number of visitors divided by the proportionate change in price – is around –0.5. (Thus a 1 per cent increase in price generates a 0.5 per cent decline in the number of visitors.) The implication of this finding is that the museum could increase its prices without reducing its revenue, despite the fact that there would be some fall off in visitor numbers. (Whether it wished to go down such a route would depend on its objectives.) Second, visitor demand is highly sensitive to income. (The income elasticity of demand is 4.3; thus a 1 per cent increase in income generates a 4.3 per cent increase in visitor numbers.) Thus as incomes grow, visitor numbers are likely to rise more than proportionately (AV_2 in Figure 1 shifts to the right). Table 2 provides some support for this proposition at the aggregate level. Finally, increases in quality have a positive effect on numbers.

The analysis undertaken by Darnell *et al.* was necessarily limited in scope because of a lack of suitable data. It did not, for instance, incorporate travel costs into the admission price. These costs are perceived by visitors as part of the overall cost of visiting the museum and may sometimes be substantial. In the absence of repeat visits they are likely to become an increasingly important element in the price as the museum tries to attract customers from further and further afield. Furthermore, the model does not incorporate marketing behaviour as an explanatory variable, nor is any allowance made for reactions by *other* museums to price and quality changes. The complex issue of the determinants of repeat visits was not addressed, even though such visits may be crucial to the growth of visitor numbers. It might be expected that a visitor's experience of the museum would 'decay' as the period since the last visit lengthens. At some stage the experience will have decayed to such an extent that the visitor is willing to make a repeat visit. The willingness to make such visits may also be affected by marketing and/or developments in the quality of the experience offered.

The visitor demand schedule facing any given museum is unlikely to remain static. Visitor tastes change and innovation occurs. The London Science Museum has estimated (HMSO, 1989b: xii) that the average life of a gallery in a modern science museum is between ten and twelve years, and sometimes shorter. Experience in the early 1980s at Beamish (Johnson and Thomas, 1990a) showed the adverse effect on visitor numbers that can be generated by the absence of continued product development.

'Social' demand

It has long been acknowledged by economists that the 'private' demand reflected in AV_2 in Figure 1 may not always be an accurate reflection of the wider 'social' demand for the benefits of museums. Some elements which may not be captured in private demand are briefly considered below.

Option demand   This demand is most relevant in terms of the visitor experience. Some individuals may wish to preserve (and be willing to pay for) the *option* of visiting a museum at some future date, even though in the event they may choose not to exercise that option. Such people place an *option value* (Hughes, 1989) on the visitor experience. The option value argument may be extended to include instances where individuals wish to preserve the possibility that *others* can visit the museum. The provision of visitor experience options has a public good element. If the option is provided for one, then (up to capacity limits) it is provided for others. Thus there is non rivalry in consumption. Non-excludability also characterizes the option, although an *actual* visit would be excludable.

Some individuals who have an option demand may decide to visit the museum not because they derive utility from the visit *per se* but in order to make some contribution through admission charges, if they exist, to the upkeep of the museum, thereby ensuring that it is kept open and that their future options are preserved. (Even if there is no admission charge, their visit conveys a signal of continuing demand for the museum.) Alternatively they may send a donation, or offer voluntary help. Thus there may already be some expression of option demand through the private market system.

Spillover demand We have already indicated that there may be positive spillover effects from museum activities. It is possible that some of these spillover benefits will be reflected in various kinds of payments to the museum from beneficiaries; where they are not, only some form of public intervention can ensure optimality in resource allocation.

Merit good demand Governments may judge that output which would not be provided through the private market and which does not generate spillover effects is nevertheless desirable in some way and should therefore be provided. They may for example believe that individuals should be able to enjoy a particular type of experience which is not currently on offer. Where a visitor experience is already available, governments may want to encourage individuals – either generally or from particular sections of society – to have that experience, even though those individuals may not wish to go. (Such unwillingness may of course arise even where there is no admission charge.) Again, the provision of scholarly work on museum collections may be deemed desirable from a cultural viewpoint. These arguments all view museum output as a 'merit' good. (For a discussion of such goods in a related context see Netzer, 1978: 26–7, and Throsby and Withers, 1979: 196–202). Layard and Walters (1978: 25 fn) argue that merit goods arise because of a lack of information: if people knew the true level of satisfaction that would be generated by a visitor experience, they would demand it for themselves, and government would have no role to play.

Demand by future generations If the demands of future generations both for scholarly output and visitor experiences are to be met, it may be necessary, as suggested above (p. 22), to register that demand in the current generation, e.g. to ensure that artefacts are collected and preserved. Some of this demand may, in fact, already be registered by private individuals in the ways previously described, but it may also be necessary for governments to 'buy' more current museum output to ensure provision for future generations.

Public funding

One of the main grounds on which a general case for the public funding of museums may be argued was suggested in the previous section: private demand may not fully reflect social demand.

However, it is important to stress that some of the social demands that may at first appear not to be expressed in a private market system, may, in fact, be reflected to some degree in a range of money and 'in kind' payments. On the other hand, where museum output is characterized by non-excludability, some individuals may attempt to 'free ride', i.e. to receive the benefits without paying. To the extent that private demand fail to reflect the true social demand, a private market system would deliver an output level that is socially sub-optimal.[6]

It is important to realize that even though such 'market failure' may occur this fact in itself is not enough to justify public funding, since the latter may induce 'goverment failure' which more than offsets the gains from eliminating market failure. Government failure for our purposes may be taken to include failure not only in sponsoring ministries and agencies but also in museum managements. A possible source of government failure may be the development of managerial slack arising from the availability of public funds. The requirement to follow the bureaucratic procedures often associated with public funding may sometimes stifle innovative behaviour. Also, managements may wish to maximize the total budget they receive from their funding agencies because salaries and prestige are related to the size of that budget. The achievement of such a goal is unlikely to be consistent with the maximization of social welfare.

Resource allocation

Some preliminary issues

Objectives Any judgement on how well resources are allocated must, of course, be made against specified criteria. Which criteria are used will depend on the purpose of the evaluation exercise. Different interest groups will wish to apply different criteria. For instance, the Treasury may be concerned with the effects of different resource allocations in the museum sector on Exchequer costs, while museum managements may be more concerned with effects on the quality of their scholarship and displays, visitor numbers or museum accounts.

A criterion often used in economic analysis is social efficiency. Such efficiency is maximized when the excess of all the social benefits over all the social costs is maximized. This criterion has intuitive appeal at the level of society as a whole. However, it may conflict with other criteria, such as purely commercial considerations. This possibility may be demonstrated with reference to Figure 1 (p. 26). Let us assume that a museum is trying to maximize its net income (i.e. total revenue minus total costs) and charges a price of P_1. Let us further assume that at this price the museum cannot pay its way (net income is negative). On a commercial criterion the museum should shut down, and the resources be reallocated elsewhere. However, a different outcome might result if account were taken of all the social benefits derived from the museum's existence. Let us assume that the total gross social benefit from the museum may be measured by the 'willingness to pay' of all the visitors presented in Figure 1. (There are no spillover benefits of the kind described on p. 29). In Figure 1 the total willingness to pay of all those who would visit at price P_1, i.e. V_1 visitors, is ABV_10. It is clear that this is greater than the amount actually paid which is P_1BV_10. The difference is the consumers' surplus, which definitionally gives rise to no financial flow to the museum or its sponsoring authorities. Nevertheless, it is possible that this surplus may be greater than any deficit incurred by the museum. We have shown elsewhere (Johnson and Thomas, 1990a) that in the case of Beamish, consumers' surplus more than covers the revenue loss. Thus even in the absence of externalities the museum's existence generates positive net social benefits.

Figure 1 also demonstrates another possible conflict of criteria: visitor numbers are maximized at V_2 with a zero price. Such a price, though, would generate a higher financial loss than a positive price. It would also reduce net social benefits.[7]

Social efficiency *versus* equity A socially efficient allocation of resources may be variously distributed. How this distribution is made depends on 'equity' considerations. The latter are briefly examined on pp. 33–34. The next section looks more closely at social efficiency.

Social efficiency

Some basic rules Social efficiency requires efficiency at different levels. First, there is the allocation of resources to museums rather than to other activities in the economy; second, there is the allocation of resources between different museums (and between different outputs of museums); and, third, there is the question of the efficient mix of resources (e.g. staff of various skills, buildings, collections and capital equipment) in each museum. At all these levels it can be shown that social efficiency will be maximized where marginal social benefit (i.e. the addition to social benefit arising from a unit increase in the relevant activity) is equal to marginal social cost (i.e. the addition to total social cost arising from a unit increase in the relevant activity).[8] To operate at less than this level means that more could be added to social benefits than to social cost by expanding; to go beyond this level means that more is being added to costs than to benefits. Such a principle may be applied to questions concerning the allocation of resources to museums as a whole as well as between and within museums: socially efficient allocation implies that it is not possible to increase total net benefit by switching resources between museums or between outputs or functions within museums. This in turn means that the marginal social benefit from a unit of resource should be equalized in all uses.

Contingent valuation   While theoretical principles are relatively easy to expound, their application raises considerable problems. A key reason for such difficulty is that many social costs and benefits are not readily measured and then evaluated in money terms. Some difficulties on the costs side have already been mentioned above (p. 23). However, it is on the benefits side, that the problems are particularly acute. The difficulties arise in part because of the public good nature of some museum output.

One technique which has been developed in recent years to capture the benefits of public goods, particularly in the environmental field (McConnell, 1985) is that of contingent valuation. Surveys of the general public are used to ascertain the monetary valuation placed by individuals on the provision of public goods. Responses are contingent upon a hypothetical market existing for such goods. Such an approach faces a number of conceptual and empirical difficulties. One such difficulty is the possibility that responses may be distorted by 'strategic bias': given the public good nature of some museum output, a respondent has an incentive not to disclose his or her true valuation. A full discussion is contained in Throsby and Withers, 1979; these authors show *inter alia* the conditions under which overstatement or understatement for a public good may occur. There is a substantial debate on how important strategic bias is; some economists have taken issue with the conventional wisdom, arguing that it may not exist or that if it does, it is empirically insignificant: again Throsby and Withers have a good review of relevant studies. Their own study of the arts in Sydney, Australia, suggested that the free rider problem does exist and that it is significant. They also suggested ways of overcoming bias in empirical studies.

Another difficulty is that even if respondents are honest in their responses, they may not be fully informed at the time they participate in the survey about the nature of museum output. Furthermore, society as a whole may have a perspective which is different from that of the individuals that make it up. Thus the merit good argument in so far as it is not based on information deficiencies alone, is unlikely to be fully captured through this approach.

A respondent's valuation is likely to be affected by his or her income. The results of any survey are therefore only relevant for the income distribution that existed among respondents at the time it was conducted. However, there is no reason why these results should not be used to *simulate* the effects on the aggregate valuation placed on public goods of different income distributions.

Equity issues

Typically, in discussions of equity, economists are interested in the distribution of goods, or access to them, across individuals and households, ranked by income level. This is often the concern for example in discussions of the equity aspects of pricing. A separate, though nevertheless, interesting, further aspect of distribution is that across individuals or households in different geographical locations. Some basic data on this latter issue are given in Table 8. Two features of this table stand out. The first is the fairly close similarity in estimated *total* spending per head between the three mainland countries (third column) although it should be noted that there are significant variations in the distribution of expenditure as between central and local governments. The second is the much lower total expenditure per head in Northern Ireland which is largely accounted for by the very low figure for local government.

Table 8, however, disguises significant geographical variations in public support for museums *within* each constituent country of the United Kingdom. In England, for example, the NMGs are concentrated in London. In Scotland the Museum and Galleries Commission (1988: 12) has shown that while 'the overall distribution of museums follow in a rough and ready manner that of population' there is nevertheless 'a striking imbalance in distribution when the nature and quality of collections are taken into account'. There are, of course, ways of spreading the benefits more evenly: travelling exhibitions,

Table 8   *Geographical distribution of public sector funding for museums*

	Central government expenditure per head, 1988/9 (pence)	Local government expenditure per head 1987/8 (pence)	Estimated total expenditure per head 1988/89 prices (pence)[b]
England	342	187	538
Scotland	290[a]	278	596
Wales	414	145	566
Northern Ireland	350	38	387
TOTAL UK	283	189	481

Source: Policy Studies Institute, 1989: 4.
Notes:
[a] 1987/8
[b] The figures in the second column have been increased by 5 per cent. The central goverment figure for Scotland in column 1 has also been increased by the same percentage.

loans of national treasures to other museums, and 'outstations' are possibilities. Some benefits of the museums can be also obtained without a visit, through television or publications, for instance. But it would be difficult to escape the conclusion that certain groups, such as people living in the South East, have a better opportunity to take advantage of the NMGs. It should be noted that one of the aims of current policy is to make the 'arts' (here including museums) 'more available to people living in all parts of the country' (HMSO, 1989c: 2).

Two other questions relevant to the distribution issue may also be mentioned. The first concerns how far overseas visitors should receive a subsidy when visiting United Kingdom museums. Important aspects of this question are the extent to which the subsidy is reciprocated when UK residents travel abroad and the scale of spin-off benefits generated by overseas visitors who are attracted to this country by the existence of (subsidized) museums. The second question relates to the distribution of costs and benefits across generations. We have already seen that conflicts of interest between generations may arise. The only way in which such conflicts can be resolved is through some weighting mechanism. Unfortunately different interest groups are likely to propose different weights.

Pricing

There is now an extensive debate on charging admission to museums.[9] This debate has focused most recently on admission to the NMGs (HMSO, 1989b) [10] The following discussion should therefore be seen in this context.

There are at least two levels at which the effects of pricing on resource allocation may be discussed. First, does the introduction of admission charges raise or lower the resources available to the NMGs? Second, what effect does pricing have on social efficiency? We examine both issues below. We also look briefly at some other effects that might result from the introduction of admission charges. However, before we examine the *effects* of the charges, it is worth noting that it is far from clear what objectives the museums are following in introducing and then selecting the level of prices. It would be helpful to know what these are.

Pricing and the museums sector's resources

In the absence of any consequent changes in other sources of income, the introduction of admission charges will raise income, by the amount of the revenue raised less the costs of collection, and thereby increase the ability of the museums to buy in more resources. In terms of Figure 1 (p. 26) an admission price of P_1 will generate a revenue addition of P_1BV_10. This amount less collection costs will be available for additional spending.

Some commentators have argued that the amount raised by admission charges has so far been quite modest[11] but this outcome reflects the result of the *particular* level of charges imposed.[12] If the evidence from Beamish is any guide, revenues could be increased by raising prices still further. It must also be remembered that in the longer run, when the 'shock' of imposing a charge has been removed, visitor numbers may to some extent recover and revenues will thus be increased even if prices remain constant.

Whether other sources of income would, in fact, remain unaffected by the introduction of charges is unclear. Governments under financial pressure may reduce their own funding to take account of revenues from the market place. It may also be argued that the introduction of charges may reduce revenues if it leads to benefactors reducing their contributions on the grounds that the museum no longer needs outside assistance or that pricing is incompatible with the objectives behind the benefaction.[13] Volunteers may also be less willing to give their time and energy. Furthermore, the inevitable loss of visitors is likely to reduce sales of publications and revenue from catering services. Visitors who do continue to come may make compensating reductions in their purchases in the museum shops and restaurants. At present, the overall effects of charging on income are not known.

Pricing and social efficiency

The case against charging in NMGs is usually argued on the grounds that the NMGs are part of the national heritage to which all should have access irrespective of ability or willingness to pay. People should be encouraged, not deterred, from visiting their national museums. Furthermore, admission charges are seen as discouraging repeat visits which are important for a full appreciation of the collections.

This argument may be examined with reference to Figure 1. The introduction of a charge of P_1 reduces visitor numbers from V_2 to V_1 in the current period. (The fall in visitor numbers in the NMGs since the introduction of charges is documented in Policy Studies Institute, 1989: 6). If P_1 reflects (constant) marginal social costs and if the private demand schedule AV_2 represents marginal social benefits, then V_1 will be the socially optimal output (marginal social cost equals marginal social benefit). Those visitors represented by the section BV_2 on the demand schedule value a visit at less than the social cost of provision. Those visitors who are not put off by the charge receive less consumers' surplus than previously, but they could *in principle* be compensated by the recipients of the proceeds of the admission charges, assuming no collection costs. There is, therefore, no overall loss in social welfare as far as these visitors are concerned, although the distribution of that welfare has changed. It should be noted that if the Beamish cost data given on pp. 24–25 above are typical and if the private costs actually paid by the museum reflect social costs, then the socially optimal price at least up to capacity limits will be very low since marginal costs are low.

The opponents of pricing would of course argue that AV_2 does not reflect the true social demand, once merit good and spillover arguments are taken into account. In their view non-visitors should be encouraged to attend, and those that do visit, to do so more often. 'Free days' – such as Fridays at the Imperial War Museum – may go some way towards meeting this objective but they do little for those who have restricted flexibility in their visiting times. There may be other ways of combining a pricing system with the achievement of wider objectives. For example, the state might pay the admission charges on behalf of certain groups. Such a system would have the advantage of ensuring that the resource costs of meeting social objectives is clearly identifiable although it might be complex to administer and be subject to some abuse.

Although the introduction of admission charges may induce a reduction of visitor numbers in the *current* period (in terms of Figure 1, there is a movement up AV_2), it may, if it raises the total income available to the museum, enhance the quality of its collections and thereby raise visitor numbers in *subsequent* periods above what they would otherwise be (in terms of Figure 1, AV_2 will shift to the right). Thus there may be a trade-off between the loss in visitor numbers in the current period and the gain in such numbers in later periods. In such cases any discussion of the effects of pricing on numbers should be explicit about the terms on which this trade-off is being made.

Other effects of price

It has just been argued that the introduction of an admission charge may affect the quality of the product if an increase in income is used to improve collections. The quality of the visitor experience may also be raised by admission charges if, as a result, visitors become more determined to obtain value for money. Furthermore, it may provide important signals which, when carefully interpreted, may stimulate managers and policymakers to change their strategies. For example a dramatic fall off in visitor numbers following the introduction of charges does at least raise *prima facie* questions concerning the nature of the collections on offer and whether they could (and should) be made more attractive to potential visitors. Such a fall can also force managements to be more precise about why public funding in such circumstances is justified.

Conclusions

In this paper we have briefly examined various aspects of resource allocation in museums. The issues are complex and the contribution that the economist can make must be combined with that from other perspectives. However, there is no escaping the fact that most resources do have alternative uses. The allocation of resources to and within the museums sector is therefore a legitimate area for economic research. Such research should not assume that because a particular allocation currently exists, it is necessarily optimal. At the same time, it is likely that any contribution that the economist can make will be fairly narrowly defined and be concerned with evaluating actual or potential marginal adjustments. Nevertheless, given the relative absence of existing work, even a modest research programme could yield substantial value added. A first priority is to ensure that a consistent database on resource use in museums is maintained and developed. The Policy Studies Institute and the Museums Association have made a very useful start, but their efforts need to be maintained and developed, particularly as much assistance to the museums sector is either hidden or diffused through a wide variety of funding agencies.

On the benefits side, detailed work on the wider benefits of museum activities, perhaps using a contingent valuation approach, could be fruitful and build on work already undertaken in the performing arts. The distribution of costs and benefits, both geographically and across different income groups in the population, also needs to be studied in greater depth. In this context, it would be valuable to undertake an objective study of the impact on social benefits of the introduction of admission charges in NMGs.

Research on both costs and benefits could usefully gain from international comparative work. Comparisons across institutions are unlikely to be easy but the careful collection and interpretation of data could provide a useful input into management and policy decisions.

Notes

1. This paper is part of a larger project being undertaken by the authors into the economic impact of the North of England Open Air Museum at Beamish. The authors are grateful to the Joseph Rowntree Memorial Trust for their financial assistance and to Peter Lewis, Museum Director at Beamish, and his staff for their advice and cooperation. All errors and omissions, however, are the sole responsibility of the authors.
2. The NMGs as a category are not identical with the 'national and government department museums' grouping in Table 1, but there is extensive overlap.

3. Gross domestic product at market prices at 1985 factor cost: *UK National Accounts 1989*, Table 1.6.
4. Report of the Chief Officers to Durham County Council Museums Sub Committee, 7 September 1965.
5. In terms of Figure 1, this model considers the effect of both *movement along* the demand schedule (caused by changes in price alone) and *shifts in* that schedule (caused by changes in such factors as income, weather and quality).
6. As shown on p. 23 *private costs* may not accurately reflect *social* costs. A market allocation based on the former costs will also lead to sub-optimality in resource allocation. The divergence between private and social costs is however likely to be less of a problem than the divergence between private and social benefits. Thus, only the latter is considered here.
7. This is because the addition to total costs resulting from a movement from V_1 to V_2 would be greater than the addition to total benefit measured by the area BV_1V_2.
8. It is also necessary for the marginal social cost schedule to cut the marginal social benefit schedule from below. The discussion in the text makes the further implicit assumption that the marginal conditions in *all other parts of the economy* are met. If this is not the case, then it may not follow that satisfying these conditions in the museum sector alone will raise social welfare overall. For a discussion of this 'second best' problem see Layard and Walters (1978: 180f).
9. This debate is not new: charges for museums and galleries were first proposed in 1970: see Peacock and Godfrey (1974). See also Elkan (1986).
10. For opposing views among NMG Directors on pricing see N. McGregor, 'Charge that would be self defeating', *The Times*, 16 December 1989, and A. Borg, 'Money is no object', *The Times*, 2 January 1990.
11. See, for example, R. Simon, 'To charge or not to charge...or both', *Independent*, 21 January 1990.
12. Where the price elasticity of demand is unity, the revenue collected will be the same whatever the price charged.
13. This argument was put by the National Gallery to the Education, Science and Arts Committee of the House of Commons: see HMSO, 1989b: viii–ix.

Bibliography

Darnell, A.C., Johnson, P.S. and Thomas, R.B., 'Modelling Visitor Flows: A Case Study of Beamish Museum', *Tourism Management* 10(2): 251–7, 1990.

40 *Museum economics and the community*

Elkan, W., 'Collecting for Galleries and Museums', *National Westminster Bank Quarterly Review*, February 1986: 26–36.

English Tourist Board, *Sightseeing 1988* (London, 1989).

HMSO, *Department of Education and Science and Office of Arts and Libraries Expenditure Plans, 1989–90 to 1991–92*, Education and Science Committee, Second Report, HC369, Session 1988–89 (HMSO: London, 1989a).

HMSO, *Should Museums Charge? Some Case Studies*, Education, Science and Arts Committee, First Report, HC351, Session 1988–9, and HC94, Session 1989–90 (HMSO, London, 1989b).

HMSO, *The Government's Expenditure Plans 1989–90 to 1991–92; Chapter 13: Office of Arts and Libraries*, HM Treasury, Cm613 (HMSO: London, 1989c).

Hughes, G., 'Measuring the Economic Value of the Arts', Policy Studies Institute 9 (3) (London, 1989): 33–45.

Johnson, P.S., Thomas, R.B., 'The Development of Beamish: An Assessment', *International Journal of Museum Management and Curatorship* 9(1): 5–24, 1990a.

Johnson, P.S. and Thomas, R.B., 'Measuring the Local Impact of a Tourist Attraction: An Empirical Study', *Regional Studies* 24(5): 395–403, 1990b.

Lyard, P.R.G. and Walters, A.A., *Microeconomic Theory* (McGraw Hill: New York and Maidenhead, 1978).

McConnell, K.E., 'The Economics of Outdoor Recreation' in *Handbook of Natural Resource and Energy Economics* A.V. Kneese and J.L. Sweeney (Eds), II (Amsterdam, 1985): 677–722.

Museums Association, *Museums UK. The Findings of the Museums Data-Base Project* (Museums Association: London, 1987a).

Museums Association, *Museums UK The Findings of the Museums Data-Base Project: Update 1* (Museums Association: London, 1987b).

Museums and Galleries Commission, *Museums in Scotland: Report by a Working Party* (HMSO: London, 1986).

Museums and Galleries Commission, *The National Museums* (HMSO: London, 1988).

Myerscough, J., *The Economic Importance of the Arts in Britain*, Policy Studies Institute 672 (London, 1988).

Netzer, D., *The Subsidized Muse* (Cambridge University Press: Cambridge, 1978).

Peacock, A. and Godfrey, C., 'The Economics of Museums and Galleries', *Museums Journal* 74 (2) 1974: 55–8.

Policy Studies Institute, *Cultural Trends No. 4* (London, 1989).

Robbins, L., 'Art and the State', in *Politics and Economics* Robbins L. (ed.) (Macmillan: London, 1963): 53–72.

Throsby, C.D. and Withers, G.A., *The Economics of the Performing Arts*, (Edward Arnold, London, 1979).

2

Performance indicators: promises and pitfalls

PETER M. JACKSON

Introduction

In 1989 about £300 million of public expenditure was allocated to national and local museums in the UK. A basic question is, did the tax payer receive value for money from this expenditure? How well are museums managed?

To answer questions of this kind it is now customary to measure the performance of museums by means of performance indicators. This is not, however, a straightforward technical procedure: it is full of problems and pitfalls for the unwary. The apparent technical sophistication of performance measurement is a mask which can hide conflicting values and deep-rooted conceptual issues such as what is performance, and what is meant by value for money?

This essay reviews a number of the conceptual, measurement and behavioural problems which those who engage in performance measurement and performance review should be aware of. Without an appreciation of these issues a blind application of managerialist prescriptions could have the unintended effect of depreciating the performance of museums.

Why performance measurement?

The financial climate within which public sector museums in the UK have to operate has become more hostile in recent years. From the mid-1970s the objective of successive governments has been to contain public expenditure increases. This has resulted in reductions in budgets (in real terms) and a greater emphasis placed upon the market place as an alternative source of income. Museums have not escaped these general changes in public expenditure policy. Local authority museums rely heavily upon grants from local government: about 16 per cent of their incomes comes from the 'market place' through earned sources. Independent museums have not escaped these financial pressures. A survey carried out by the Museums Association found that 42 per cent of the income of independent museums came from public grants in 1985 (Myerscough, 1986, 1988).

Irrespective of whether museums are located in the public or the private sector of an economy, the financial environment which they face is extremely uncertain. In the future the operating grants for UK museums are likely to remain constant. Any developments will, therefore, need to be resourced either from cost savings within existing budgets or from the generation of additional incomes earned from the market place. This will not be an easy task. Labour costs account for over 50 per cent of museums' operating budgets. There is, however, little scope for productivity increases in labour intensive organizations such as museums. The managers of museums, given this general background now need to pay closer attention to the performance of their budgets. Are existing museum activities and services providing value for money? Are current resources being allocated efficiently and effectively? To answer these questions managers need measures and indicators of their performance.

For many organizations, such as museums, the bottom line of profit, which is frequently used as the ultimate test of performance, does not exist. This is true for public sector museums and for those private museums which are organized on a 'not-for-profit' basis. In these cases both financial performance and the impact of services are difficult to measure. Nevertheless, it is important to know if museums' resources are being allocated efficiently and if they are being employed in such a way that will have maximum effect. Managers of museums require information on efficiency and effectiveness if they are to evaluate the performance of their organizations. This information is provided through performance indicators. Without the information provided by performance indicators, managers are in danger of allocating resources 'in the dark'. The management of one museum will not know how their performance compares with that of other similar museums or how their own performance has changed over time. Without such information they will not know when diagnostic investigations of their current management practices will be necessary.

Performance measurement contributes to a number of management's activities:

(1) it assists in the formation and implementation for policy;
(2) it assists in the planning and budgeting of service provision and in the monitoring of the implementation of planned change;
(3) it helps to improve the standards of service content and of organizational effectiveness;
(4) it helps in the review of the efficient use of resources;
(5) it is used to increase control and influence over decision making.

Performance measurement improves management practice. It provides essential information to management by enabling activities to be monitored on a regular basis at several levels within the organization. Performance measurement also provides information for strategy post-mortems when policies, management practices, and methods are evaluated.

A survey of the current use of performance measures in UK local authorities, carried out by the Public Sector Economics Research Centre at Leicester University, found that managers regarded the best features of performance measures to be:

(a) the ability to make comparisons of actual performance against targets; against performance in a previous period; or against the performance of similar departments or programmes;
(b) the ability to highlight areas of interest and the relevant questions to ask;
(c) the ability to provide a broad ranging picture of a service;
(d) the identification of trends over time;
(e) the development of local bench marks, norms or targets (Jackson and Palmer, 1989).

The use of performance measures is, therefore, an essential management tool. Performance measures provide the information which managers require to enhance the performance of their organization. Some, however, see performance measures exclusively in the context of improving managerial control. Information is a means of exercising control and strengthening accountability. It cannot be denied that performance measures can and should be used in this way but to focus on the control aspects is to run the danger of performance measurement being regarded with suspicion and to invoke undesirable responses to its introduction. There is a more positive aspect to the use of performance measurement; it enables organizational learning. If actual performance falls short of a pre-set target then management can ask the question, 'Why was there a short-fall?' and learn from the answer provided.

Performance measurement is, therefore, necessary for accountability and control but it is also essential for organizational learning which is, in turn, necessary for improving the performance of the organization. The measurement of performance must take place within a framework and it is to such a framework that attention is now given.

Concepts and framework for performance measurement

An organization such as a museum can be thought of as a system which is dependent for its resources upon its relationships with the external environment. Public sector museums are heavily dependent upon their relationships with sponsoring central and local government departments. Private and 'not-for-profit' museums depend upon the market place, private sponsors and benefactors. Clearly, the system of mixed public and private finance which now characterizes UK public sector museums involves a complex web of resource dependency relationships. This means that there are a number of different constituencies whose interests museum managers seek to satisfy. It is not inconceivable that these interests will at times come into conflict with one another. Management is faced with the task of choosing which interests to serve at the expense of others or to seek a reconciliation of interests. All constituencies will wish to be satisfied that they are receiving value for money. Performance is, therefore, evaluated within a value-for-money framework (VFM).

Museums, like any other organization, use their resources to purchase inputs (labour and capital, e.g. buildings, materials) in order to provide an output or a service which clients/customers demand. The value-for-money framework essentially examines the performance of a museum in terms of the relationship between its resources inputs and its service outputs while at the same time seeking to establish whether or not the service outputs that are being provided are those which are valued by the museum's various constituencies.

There are three fundamental elements to the value-for-money framework which are commonly referred to as the 'Three Es'. These are economy, efficiency and effectiveness:

Economy is concerned with minimizing the cost of resources acquired or used, having regard to the quality of the inputs. In short, economy is about spending less;

Efficiency is concerned with the relationship between the output of goods, services or other results and the resources used to produce them. How far is maximum output achieved for a given input, or minimum input used for a given output? In short, efficiency is about spending well;

Effectiveness is concerned with the relationship between the intended results and the actual results of the projects programmes and services. How successfully do the outputs of goods, services or other results achieve policy objectives, operational goals and other intended effects? In short, effectiveness is about spending wisely.

The value-for-money framework as set out above, has been developed in the UK by the National Audit Office, which is responsible for ensuring that central government funds are being spent in a way that maximizes performance as measured by the Three Es. The Audit Commission for England and Wales and the Accounts Commission for Scotland serve a similar function for local government public expenditures.

In reality, the boundaries between economy, efficiency and effectiveness are seldom clear cut. Nevertheless, this troika does provide the basis for a VFM examination. For example, a VFM examination of museums might cover any or all of the following aspects:

(1) the tendering, contract, project control procedures, used for capital construction work; the purchasing procedures used for acquisitions and the purchase of materials. This will give management information about whether or not purchasing is being carried out at the best possible set of prices consistent with the desired quality of inputs (Economy);

(2) utilization of facilities; staff allocations and mix, integration of services; maintenance; management and resource allocation systems (Efficiency);

(3)   results in terms of consumer satisfaction; improved educa-
       tional value; improved awareness of a nation's cultural
       heritage etc. (Effectiveness).

Managers of museums should have as their objective the maximization of value added. The VFM framework enables them to demonstrate whether or not they are achieving this objective.

Clearly, some of those who come from a non-managerialist culture
will challenge the values contained in the above normative statement
that the managerial objective is to maximize value added. Some
might even feel that their professional values are threatened by such
an approach. A moment's reflection should, however, reveal that the
values of museum professionals can be consonant with the managerialist values. This is not to deny that the approach is not without
its own problems, which will be explored at greater length later in this
paper.

Value added is simply the difference between the value of a
museum's inputs and its outputs. Problems arise with the notion of
value added because it is very difficult to obtain information about
the value placed upon the outputs of museum services – especially
when there is no market test, such as how much individuals are
willing to pay to obtain these services, as in the case of private sector
museums.

Minimization of the value of inputs is a relatively straightforward
task for managers seeking to maximize value added. It is an exercise
in cost minimization and budget restraint. However, both sides of the
equation are not independent. An over-zealous attempt to contain
costs can spill over into a reduction in the quality of the output
(services) with the result that the valuation of that output falls also.
Cost containment is, therefore, not necessarily consistent with the
maximization of value added. Attention has to be given to the
valuation of the service provided. Not only are there measurement
problems such as how to place a monetary value on an intangible
service that is not traded in the market place but there are conceptual
problems to be addressed also. Whose values are to count? This is
another way of asking the questions, who are the consumers of
museums' services; who are the custodians of their values?

Asking questions of this kind, within a VFM framework, throws
into relief those issues which some museum workers might regard to
be threatening to their set of professional values. For some time now

throughout the public sector (and indeed the independent sector) there has been a growing view that it has been the interests of professional monopoly suppliers that have dominated the design of service levels, quality and mix rather than those of the consumer or tax payer. Service providers have failed to take sufficiently into account the views of their customers or when those views are sought they have tended to override them.

There are two distinct dimensions to the VFM framework. One focuses upon minimizing the cost of inputs; whatever service is produced should be produced at minimum cost consistent with quality constraints. The other dimension, which is usually forgotten, requires that the service which is produced is, in fact, valued by those who use it. There is no rationality in producing something at minimum cost if no one wants it. The VFM framework places the values of consumers back into the managerial decision about determining service levels, mixes and qualities. Obtaining information about consumers' preferences and their evaluations of services is no mean task. Indeed, many professional groups would question the worth that should be placed upon such information. These are valid responses but what should be recognized is that by paying attention to consumers' wishes, these problems are brought into the open.

In the case of museum services many – perhaps most – consumers do not know what they want and having experienced the service they do not know what valuation to place upon it. A customer-centred management will, however, seek to find out what its customers think of the services that it is providing. Rather than simply taking the attitude, 'we are the professionals and know best', a customer-centred service will approach the problem in a variety of ways, paying attention to the need to educate the public to value aspects of their cultural heritage; to find out what consumers find appealing; to learn about why some consumers visit museums whilst others do not. This in turn requires performance indicators on service usage and it is an example of how performance indicators can be used as a means of organizational learning. If, as a result of changing the type of services provided by a museum, attendance figures increase significantly, then this is an indication that consumer interests are being served and that value has been added.

There can be a tendency to make use of elaborate customer surveys using questionnaires or to seek information about consumer complaints. While these approaches can be useful means of obtaining

information about customer evaluations of the service they are not
without problems that museum managers should be aware of. First,
they can be expensive to organize. To obtain value for money from
such information means that the value of the information obtained
should outweigh the cost of obtaining it. This requires attention and
care to be given to the design of questions. Second, many consumers'
complaints arise not from the fact that there is anything wrong with
the level or quality of the service but because consumers hold a
misguided set of expectations. The fault lies with the consumer and
not with the producer. In that case there is a strong case for the
producer to educate the consumer and, thereby, to change consumer
expectations. Third, relying only on 'complaints' information can
give a biased view of consumer satisfaction. It is found from market
surveys of consumers generally that only 20 per cent (on average) of
those who are dissatisfied with a service will complain. This means
that complaints data need to be multiplied up by a factor of 5 to give a
realistic picture of consumer attitudes.

Beyond the Three Es

The basic VFM framework established above argues for judging the
performance of organizations in terms of whether or not they are
achieving economy, efficiency, or effectiveness. This also requires the
collection of data on consumer evaluations of services. Some,
however, argue that this approach focuses upon a very narrow
concept of performance. There are other equally important dimensions to performance which also need to be evaluated.

Here are other categories of performance which have been
suggested for inclusion in the VFM framework.

Equity: this concept raises a number of interesting problems which
are not adequately captured in the narow VFM framework. Some
services might have as one of their objectives the targeting of the
service to specific user groups. If such groups have a lower average
valuation for the service then, by definition, achieving the equity
objective means that some potential value added has been given up. A
trade-off exists between managerial objectives. This means that when
evaluating overall performance managers will be required to justify
their choice of trade-offs.

Equity considerations also force a further consideration of whose values are to count when calculating value added. Are the views of all customers to be treated equally? Should more weight be given to some groups compared to others? It is useful at this point to raise a question which it is easy to lose sight of in the managerialism of VFM: who are the consumers of museum services and can they be easily identified? One important group who cannot be left out of the answer to that question is future generations. Museum services are not just provided for today's consumers. Decisions taken today, however, will have significant implications for the provision of services for future generations. How are their values to be expressed and who looks after their interests?

Excellence: this brings the service quality dimension into relief. Quality has been touched upon already but following the work of Peters and Waterman (1982) customer-centred management needs to pay particular attention to the quality of service that is being provided. Total quality management and systems of quality assurance are now becoming popular managerial functions.

Crude budget cutting exercises which result in reductions in quality to levels below those regarded as acceptable by consumers add nothing to value. Again this highlights another of the trade-offs which managers face. Improved budgetary performance in terms of economy and efficiency at the expense of a reduction in quality has to be justified. A reduction in quality will only add to value if the previous level of quality was in excess of that which customers were prepared to pay. To know this, however, again requires obtaining information from consumers.

Entrepreneurship: as museum managements are increasingly being forced to seek alternative sources of finance they are having to be more imaginative and enterprising in their approaches to service provision. Entrepreneurship has been usefully defined by the economist Joseph Schumpeter as, 'creative destruction'. Old outmoded values and beliefs are discarded and replaced by new ways of thinking.

Entrepreneurship involves cultural change. For the museum professional it requires a reassessment of traditional professional values based upon a system of purely public finance to incorporate the values required for a mixed system of public and private finance. Again, incorporation of entrepreneurship will introduce another set of trade-offs. How much effort should go into seeking private market-led finance if that is at the expense of the equity objective?

Expertise: adoption of the VFM framework as the basis of managing in a high performance environment requires new managerial skills. A significant constraint upon the achievement of improved performance will be a lack of expertise among museum managers to deal with the complexities of value-for-money auditing. To overcome this, changes need to be made to the *education* programme for museum professionals.

Electability: this final dimension raises an important series of issues for public sector museums. There is a political dimension and a series of political accountabilities to be considered. These are left out of the narrow VFM framework. What is the political value placed upon museum services? What role is played by national and local politicians in ensuring the performance of museums? These questions are not confined to public sector museums. Private sector museums are also dependent upon political patronage in a variety of ways, e.g. the way in which the fiscal system treats private collections in terms of wealth taxation; the donation of works of art in lieu of taxes etc.

The extended VFM framework which incorporates equity, excellence, entrepreneurship, expertise and electability by adding them to economy, efficiency and effectiveness, brings the issues of performance measurement much closer to the reality of the management problem. There are many different dimensions to performance and the problem which faces management is to choose the appropriate trade-offs between each of the elements. In defining what is appropriate, management needs to pay attention to the views and values of a number of different constituencies each of whom judge the performance of museums according to different criteria. These constituencies will include: the users of museums, sponsors, politicians and museum professional associations. The assessment of performance is not a purely technical matter. It is value-laden. The question which remains is whose values should drive the system?

What is to be measured?

The above discussion has been general. It has attempted to sort out the different elements of performance. This is necessary before proceeding to consider measurement. While the phrase 'performance measurement' is frequently used, it is useful to distinguish between performance measures and performance indicators. Where economy, efficiency and effectiveness, and the other Es set out above, can be measured precisely and unambiguously, it is usual to talk about performance measures. However, when, as is most often the case, it is not possible to obtain a precise measure it is usual to refer to performance indicators.

Performance indicators are statistics, ratios, costs and other forms of information which illuminate or measure progress in achieving the aims and objectives of an organization as set out in its corporate plan. The use of performance indicators is an aid to good judgement and not a substitute for it. Performance indicators are provocative and suggestive. They alert managers to the need to examine the issue further. Thus, for example, the unit costs of museums as measured by the cost per employee; the cost per person admitted or whatever is not a performance measure – it does not suggest that one museum is more efficient than another because its unit costs are lower. It is instead a performance indicator since it signals to management the need to examine why the difference exists.

What form do performance measures and performance indicators take? What is, in fact, measured? In an interesting paper Ames (1991) points out that performance measurement and the use of performance indicators is an underdeveloped area among museologists. He then proceeds to suggest a number of indicators that might be used. In the UK, the Audit Commission has also made an attempt to define basic performance indicators for local authority museums (1986). Some of the indicators proposed in these two publications are now presented within the context of the VFM framework along with additional suggested indicators.

Cost indicators (economy)
- gross costs of service;
- gross costs per visitor;
- ratio of revenue to gross costs;
- conservation/curatorial expenditure;
- operating costs per visitor.

Level of resourcing indicators
These indicators will include index of revenue resources, capital

resources, equipment and buildings. Examples of indicators of
resources will include:

- the number of staff on the pay roll;
- the ratio of administrative staff to operative staff;
- the square footage of building space;
- the ratio of the square footage of space devoted to specific
  activities to the total available space.

Source of funds indicators

- the ratio of public to total income;
- the ratio of market generated income to total income;
- the ratio of income from various sources to total income.

Volume of service
These indicators are a crude signal of the demand for the service:

- number of attendances;
- attendances per day open;
- attendance trend – this year's total attendance divided by the
  average attendance for the last three years;
- days open per year;
- hours open per day;
- collection use, i.e. ratio of total number of objects exhibited over
  the number of objects in the collection.

Productivity indicators (efficiency)
Productivity indicators are available for the museum as a whole or for
specific departments or activities within the museum:

- energy efficiency – the ratio of energy costs to total square
  footage;
- per visitor gross sales income (i.e. sales income from admissions,
  shops, food, parking etc.);
- marketing efficiency – the ratio of the change in the marketing
  budget to the change in total admissions or total admissions
  income;
- shop efficiency – ratio of sales per square foot or per buyer or per
  visitor;
- fund raising efficiency – ratio of the change in
- fun raising costs to fund raising income;

– proportion of collection documented;
– proportion of budget allocated to conservation activity.

Availability of service (equity)

– low income accessibility – ratio of hours per week available free to total hours per week accessible during minimum three-month period of maximum public accessibility;
– minority attendance – ratio of annual minority attendance to total attendance;
– general accessibility – average number of hours open: per week or per week other than 9.00 a.m. to 5.00 p.m. on Monday to Friday;
– number of concessionary users;
– number of concessionary users as a proportion of total users.
– number of users in target groups as a proportion of the total number in the target group.

Quality

– exhibit maintenance – ratio of number of exhibits out of order to the total number of moving part exhibits;
– number of complaints from users;
– expertise of staff – ratio of staff training expenses to total number of staff (in full time equivalents).

Outcome indicators (effectiveness)

– results of surveys of customer's perceptions of the displays etc.

This list of performance indicators is nothing other than suggestive. It is not prescriptive, nor is it exhaustive. Given the state of the art of performance measurement in the museums service any indicator of performance needs to be tested with a view to establishing whether or not the data exist for it to be calculated; the utility of the information that it provides for management purposes; and the costs of acquiring that information relative to its utility. After a few years of testing a stock of reliable indicators should emerge.

Performance indicators are themselves of little interest or value. The information content of indicators is only realized if the latter are compared with something. This could be a set of indicators from different museums offering a similar range of services or it could be values of a single museum's own indicators taken from previous years. Variations in the indicators as between similar museums or between different years might invoke management to inquire as to the reasons for the variation.

Another way in which indicators are used is to set target values for them. If actual out-turn is below the target then a diagnostic enquiry may be set up to find out why – did some unexpected event which lay outside of the control of management cause the deviation? Were the targets set unrealistic, or was the shortfall due to poor performance on the part of the management?

It should be clear from this discussion that variances between a performance indicator and its comparators does not automatically imply poor performance. They simply give signals suggesting that further investigation is necessary. There are many different reasons for such variances and poor performance is only one.

Jackson (1988) has set out a number of criteria that can be used to judge the usefulness of performance indicators.

Consistency: the definitions used to produce the indicators should be consistent over time and between units.

Comparability: following from the requirement of consistency it is only reasonable to compare like with like.

Clarity: performance indicators should be simple, well defined, and easily understood.

Controllability: the manager's performance should only be judged (measured) for those areas that (s)he has control over.

Contingency: performance is not independent of the environment within which decisions are made: this includes the organizational structure and the management style adopted, as well as the complexity and uncertainty of the external environment.

Comprehensive: do the indicators reflect those aspects of behaviour which are important to management decisions making?

Bounded: concentrate upon a limited number of key indexes of performance. Those which are most likely to give the biggest pay-off in terms of valuable management information.

Relevance: many applications require specific performance indicators relevant to their needs and conditions. Do the indicators service these needs?

Feasibility: are the targets based upon unrealistic expectations? Can the targets be reached through reasonable actions?

Taking the first steps

The point has already been made that performance measurement is a relatively new managerial innovation within the museum service. Lessons can be learned from the experiences of other services which have embarked down this road. Initiation of a performance review exercise requires strong leadership from the top of the organization. It requires a partnership between the various constituencies within the organization between senior management, middle management, operatives, and in the case of public sector museums, between management and elected members. Without this unity of purpose, which is ground out of establishing a partnership, effort will be diverted to debates about the utility of performance review rather than getting down to the business of carrying out the review.

Strong leadership is required to bring about *cultural change* within the organization. This is essential if performance reviews are to have their desired effects. What is meant by cultural change in this context? It has already been touched upon when the notion of entrepreneurship was introduced and when the point was made that the new managerial ethos, which is implied by performance measurement, challenges certain cherished professional values. Cultural change means changing the system of beliefs and values which guide the top management team of an organization like a museum. This usually involves a change from an ethos of reactive administration (e.g. administering a museum's collection) to a more dynamic proactive management of the organization which places the needs and interests of the consumer at the centre of decision making and which judges success and performance in terms of serving consumer interests within a VFM framework. Indeed, part of the cultural change required is to accept the new language of VFM auditing and the idea of consumers who have preferences rather than passive service users.

The message of cultural change has to be transmitted throughout the whole organization, from top to bottom. It requires the establishment of total organizational commitment. Individuals, it has been found, time and time again, perform better in terms of contributing to the operations of the organizations if they know how their activities relate to the workings of the total organization. One means of achieving this is to ensure that service objectives are clarified and that these are communicated and translated into specific results and performance expectations at all levels in the organization.

Bringing about cultural change within an organization is most readily achieved through an organizational development programme in which training plays a central role. This will impart the ethos of a high performance organization while at the same time providing staff with the skills and expertise that are required to achieve improvements. Enhancement of performance requires, in most instances, a reorientation of existing practices which, in turn, demands a new set of expertise. Performance review, then, not only involves an information audit – i.e. are the appropriate performance indicators available as part of the management information system? – it also requires a skills audit. What new skills in the areas of communication, customer/client relations, financial management, human resource management, informatics, and so on, do operational staff require before improvements in performance can be secured? Senior and middle management in the organization will also require training in the development of managerial styles which emphasize the building of teams and the motivation of staff.

In most instances the new information and VFM auditing systems, which will generate the performance indicator data, will need to be negotiated into place. For some managers this will require the acquisition of negotiating skills. A top down approach, in which the new systems are imposed from above, is doomed to failure. To operate successfully the VFM approach requires data to construct performance indicators and those further down the organization will only release data of the quality required if they feel comfortable with the organizational climate within which the new systems are to be implemented. If they are introduced in a threatening fashion, which emphasizes their use as a tool of managerial control, then it is unlikely that cooperation will be forthcoming. On the other hand if they are presented as a means of organizational learning then cooperation and success is more likely.

Unless sufficient resources are allocated to the acquisition of new skills at all levels in the organization then improvements in performance will be put at risk. The new management information systems implied by the VFM framework are necessary but not sufficient for enhanced performance. These information systems are only beneficial if service managers know how to use them effectively.

Clarity of objectives

The first stage in any performance review exercise is to clarify the strategic or corporate objectives of the organization. It is these objectives which, in part, define the effectiveness dimension – indicators of effectiveness demonstrate the degree to which the organization has managed to achieve its strategic objectives. Unless the corporate objectives are clearly stated there is a high risk that the organization will sub-optimize. That is, although the constituent elements of the organization might meet their operational objectives, if they are not clear about how their actions contribute to the corporate objectives, then there is no guarantee that these strategic objectives will be achieved.

While at the most general level the strategic objective of any organization is the maximization of value added, subject to the constraint that the quality of the process through which value is added is acceptable, such a statement is too abstract to be of practical use. Moreover, some of the problems of defining value added have already been rehearsed. Strategic objectives need to be more concrete if they are to be translated into operational objectives.

Examples of the corporate objectives of a museum will include the following list:

– to meet satisfactorily the demand for its services;
– to provide services of quality;
– to develop services in line with demand;
– to carry out all statutory duties;
– to maintain charges at tolerable levels;
– to seek new sources of finance;
– to assist individuals and specified groups to develop their potential;
– to be a good and caring employer;
– to develop a performance oriented management style;
– to encourage an awareness in the general public of the visual arts and crafts, and of national and local matters of historical, cultural or scientific note;
– to ensure that there are clear policies for collection management and for targeting users;
– to ensure that special events and exhibitions relate to the stated policies;

–to ensure that the layout and quality of displays is visually
attractive and of a high standard;
– to ensure that facilities are fully utilized within policy guidelines;
– to foster the protection of primary evidence of national and local
history and natural history, and improving awareness of it.

Pitfalls and problems for performance measurement

While performance measurement undoubtedly has many benefits to
offer there are a number of pitfalls that those who use performance
indicators need to be aware of. Some of the problems of implementing performance indicators have been dealt with in previous sections.

Unless performance indicators are sufficiently robust then those
who supply the raw data for their compilation will tend to distort
information in order to present themselves in the best light. This is
especially true if the emphasis is placed upon performance review for
control purposes rather than for organizational learning. These
distorting tendencies will, therefore, reduce the value of performance
review unless they are recognized in advance. There is also a tendency
to fall into the trap of 'if it cannot be counted then it doesn't count'.
This overemphasis upon quantification can drive out qualitative
performance indicators and the unquantifiable dimensions of performance which are often more important when making decisions.

Performance indicators are a means to an end. They are an aid to
improved decision making and hence a means to enhanced performance. A situation can arise, however, where the generation of
performance indicators becomes an end in itself. So many indicators
are produced that managers suffer from information overloads:
analysis paralysis. The question is often asked, how many indicators
are required? Obviously, there is no hard and fast answer to this
question. Managers must judge how many indicators are manageable,
what is the value of the information that indicators provide, and how
much does it cost to produce the indicators. Experience suggests that
most managers use a limited set of key indicators. As one travels up
the organization, the number of indicators is reduced and they
become more general in their application and in the picture that they
reveal.

Some performance indicators overemphasize the short-term dimensions of performance. There can be a tendency to go for the 'quick fox' and thus to ignore the longer term and more enduring aspects of performance. This can be a problem if performance indicators are used for career development purposes. Not only is there the danger of distorting information as discussed above, there is also a bias for thrusting career-minded managers to concentrate upon those activities which will give them the maximum pay-offs in as short a time as possible. This can often result in an unbalanced mix of services; dissatisfied groups of consumers whose interests are not being served; and a lack of investment of resources in developing the service over the longer run.

At a more general level, managers should be aware that if performance indicators are used exclusively for control or appraisal purposes then this is likely to set up a series of behavioural responses which will have both unintended and undesirable consequences. Not only will there be an incentive to distort and to withhold information but attention will be given to the measurable dimensions of perforance at the exclusion of those aspects which are more difficult to quantify. Again, this is likely to result in an unbalanced mix of activities and consumer dissatisfaction. A crude example can be used to illustrate this general point. If performance is judged purely in terms of maximizing the number of attendances then the incentive thereby created will be to mount popular exhibitions only. This will result in a reduction in the average quality of exhibitions and will also leave dissatisfied those groups of consumers who have minority interests. Managing the use of performance indicators requires that managers are aware of these behavioural dysfunctions, and that a broad range of indicators is employed which covers different dimensions of performance, both over the long run and the short run.

Finally, there are severe problems involved with the interpretation of the statistics that are used to form performance indicators. At a basic level, a choice has to be made when using cost data between gross cost and net cost. Since net cost is a function of a museum's charging policy then variations in net cost will probably reflect differences in charging policy rather than differences in performance. Gross costs should, therefore, be used whenever possible, especially when making comparisons between museums. Per capita cost measures also present a number of problems. What is the relevant population variable that should be used to deflate the cost data? Is it the total population in a local area if it is a local authority museum which is being reviewed? Or should it be the numbers who visit the museum? Or the potential target population of museum users? Obviously, the choice of indicator will depend upon the question being asked; however, some perverse results can emerge for the unwary. For example, if the total population of one local authority is falling while that of another local authority is rising, and if each spends an identical amount on museum services, then in the first local authority per capita museum expenditure will be rising while in the second it will be falling. Does this mean that the first is less efficient than the second? Clearly not. If, however, expenditures were deflated by the number of visitors then the number of visitors to museums in local authority one is rising while in local authority two it is falling. the ranking would then be reversed.

This serves to illustrate some general problems of using ratio analysis. First, a ratio is sensitive to the choice made regarding the denominator – in this case, population. Second, a ratio will change if the numerator changes or if the denominator changes (or both changes). Examining trends in ratios over time or comparing the ratio for one museum relative to that for another is an exercise full of pitfalls. Ratios hide a great deal of useful information. To interrogate a ratio it is necessary to hold on file the absolute values for the numerator and denominator. Often this is not done which limits the usefulness of ratio analysis.

The previous example also helps to illustrate the difficulties of drawing up 'league tables' which compare the relative performances of similar museums. The rankings tend to be very unstable and are sensitive to the choice of indicators used to construct the ranking. Moreover, rankings are a snapshot of performance at a single movement in time. They wash out of the picture the dynamic aspects of performance. Different museums will be at different stages in their development cycle. One museum's expenditure in a single year might be relatively high because it is has recently invested resources in developing new services while other comparable museums incurred such expenditures many years previously.

Another problem involved with the interpretation of league tables is that it is usually the arithmetic mean which is used as a bench mark. Choice of the mean has to be justified since there are other measures of central tendency which would be more appropriate in most cases. The median, for example, takes into account the extent to which the distribution of performance indicators is skewed. Moreover, those who are below the mean or the median are not necessarily museums which are superior in performance terms. As has been demonstrated there are many dimensions to performance, including quality. The unit costs of one museum might be below average simply because it produces services of an inferior quality to those museums whose unit costs are above average.

This observation does not justify arguments for those museums whose unit costs are below average to spend more in order to raise their quality of service nor for those whose unit costs are above average to cut spending and reduce quality. These might be sensible policies, but are not necessarily so. It depends upon consumers' preferences. If consumers in the high-spending authority are perfectly satisfied with the quality of the service and are prepared to pay for it through higher local taxes or user charges then so be it – there is no inefficiency. Equally, if consumers in the low-spending authority are satisfied with the quality of service that they are provided with and are not prepared to spend more then again there is no inefficiency. League table rankings do nothing other than signal differences. It is up to management to enquire further about the reasons for these differences.

Some unresolved issues

The approach adopted in this essay has been unashamedly man-ageralist in its emphasis. This has, however, in the case of public sector museums to be balanced against the reality that there is a public service element to be taken into account and that political accountability is different in essence to the market notion of accountability to the consumer. Few would disagree that public sector organizations generally and museums in particular require a new culture: one which is open, democratic, and self-critical; one which encourages risk taking, learning and performance evaluation to replace the heavy-laden, closed bureaucratic organizations popu-lated by self-interested professional monopoly groups. Local voters and tax payers are now more critical in their expectations of the services that are supplied to them. The management literature has introduced the concept of 'listening organization' which pays attention to consumers, which opens up channels of communication between producers and consumers, and which is willing to learn about consumers' needs. These values have already been highlighted within the context of the VFM framework.

It is, however, necessary to look behind the rhetoric of managerialism and to enquire about what changes have, in fact, been made. The culture and the ethos may have changed superficially, the language used might now be different, but has anything of real substance changed? How is power in practice shifted from suppliers to consumers? What are the processes through which listening to consumers takes place? Which consumer groups are listened to? Are the disadvantaged consumers of museum services, for example, better off now than they were ten years ago? Do museum managers know who these disadvantaged groups are? Is customer care nothing other than an expensive public relations exercise? Is an appearance of listening and caring given while the customer/producer power relationship doesn't change?

A managerialism which emphasizes customer care tends to ignore that many public services, including museums, involve collective consumption rather than individual consumption. Although the consumerist movement is dominated by individualist thinking, political processes attempt to reconcile conflicting individual preferences for different types of museum services and services of differing qualities. Also, consumerism, by focusing purely on the individual consumer, ignores the external benefits of museums, that is, the benefits of living in a society which places a value on its cultural heritage. Because public sector museums are part of the political decision making process, it is reasonable to ask if local citizens are drawn into the making of local decisions which will influence local museum services. The managers of public sector museums are accountable to their citizens as well as being responsible to consumers.

In Britain local areas are becoming more diverse in terms of religious and ethnic groupings and income groupings. This diversity of preferences has to be managed (governed) and presents the managers of public services such as local museums with the problem of having to respond to the demands of a diverse set of organized interest groups. The management model often portrays the efficient high performance organization as one which responds smoothly to consumer demands in a least cost way. But in reality democracy is messy. Consumerism washes out the diversity of preferences and the conflicts of democracy (Hambleton and Hogget, 1987).

What is being argued here is that managerialist models have much insight to offer but they must be set in context to be of real value. It is not possible to transport without modification the performance framework which has been employed in the private sector and use it in public sector organizations.

Lest it be thought that these problems are exclusive to public sector museums, a moment's reflection reveals that the managers of independent and 'not-for-profit' museums face similar problems if to a lesser degree. They often have to reconcile the conflicting preferences of sponsors, trustees and different customer groups.

Finally, consideration has to be given to the role which is played by locally elected councillors in the performance review of local museums. In some local authorities it has been elected members who have initiated the performance review process. If elected members are to play an active role in setting strategic objectives, in reading and commenting upon departmental reports on performance and then acting upon them, then the cycle of committees needs, in most local authorities, to be critically reviewed. Space has to be carved out of an already overloaded timetable if members' involvement in performance review is to be anything other than token. Members, like officers and staff, also need training in the expertise required to make a contribution to performance review (Stewart, 1990).

Conclusions

Performance measurement and review is a relatively new set of activities within the world of museums management. In this essay, the value-for-money framework has been presented in an enhanced form which takes into account that performance is a multi-faceted phenomenon and that those who manage the performance of museums must make judgements about the trade-offs between the different dimensions of performance.

A number of performance indicators have been presented in a speculative way which it is hoped will stimulate further debate. the problems and pitfalls involved in implementing performance indicators have also been examined along with the limitations and unresolved issues of applying a managerialist approach to public sector organizations.

Despite these problems, pitfalls and limitations, the culture of public sector management has now changed. The challenge which faces museums management is to implement the VFM framework in a thoughtful and critical way.

Bibliography

Ames, P., 'Breaking new ground: measuring museums' merits in *Museum Management*, G. Kavanagh (ed.) (Leicester University Press: Leicester, 1991: 57–68).

Audit Commission, *Performance Review Supplement: Implementation Guide* (HMSO: London, 1966).

Hambleton, R. and Hogget, P., *Decentralisation and Democracy: localising public services*, University of Bristol, School for Advanced Urban Studies (Bristol, 1987).

Jackson, P.M., 'The Management of Performance in the Public Sector' *Public Money and Management* 8, 1988: 11–16.

Jackson, P.M. and Palmer, D.R., *First Steps in Measuring Performance in the Public Sector* (Public Finance Foundation: London, 1989).

Myerscough, J., *Facts About the Arts 2*, Policy Studies Institute 656 (London, 1986).

Myerscough, J., *The Economic Importance of the Arts in Britain*, Policy Studies Institute 672 (London, 1988).

Peters, T.J. and Waterman, R.H., *In Search of Excellence* (Harper & Row: New York, 1982).

Stewart, J., 'The Role of Councillors in the Management of the Authority' *Mimeo* 1990.

3

Sight, disability and the museum

NICH PEARSON

This essay is about vision, visual impairment, art, the work of art galleries and museums, recent developments to open up access to museums and galleries for the visually impaired, the variable nature of sight, the lack of understanding of the creative nature of seeing, a project undertaken in Wales to sensitize a group of galleries and museums to the problems and needs of people with visual impairment, and the wider context of the debate about the rights and needs of the disabled.

In preparing the essay I have written from a position that is, according to the topic both objective and subjective, involved, personal, and, I hope, informative. I can only be partisan when, for example, citing the Universal Declaration of Human Rights. I believe in *rights* rather than charity and concessions. The practice in Britain, and given with strenuous backing by the present government, has been to foster *charity*. I do not believe that because you have less sight, less hearing, limited leg movement, (or are Black, a woman, or a child of poorer parents) your opportunities in life should be less. About this I therefore write subjectively. But, as a former art officer of an arts council, I have also been directly involved in developing projects to explore and extend the opportunities of, and for, the visually impaired in experiencing museums and galleries. About this I try to write objectively. I worked with others to try to achieve certain ends. We had a measure of success. I report on that.

And then again I write about other issues to do with art, the nature of seeing and the problems of perception from both an objective and a subjective point of view. Sight is a complicated thing. I myself have poor sight. The son of an artist, and with a doctorate, a career and many publications to do with the history, practice and administration of the visual arts, I write both subjectively and objectively about many of the issues – from the inside and the outside. Objectivity is an essential, important and necessary device. It is essential to scholarship. But the denial of subjectivity is also unhelpful and obscuring.

The background

During the 1980s there was a considerable increase in interest in matters to do with museums, galleries, and the disabled (e.g. Weisen, 1988a, 1988b; Raffrey, 1988). Reports were produced, and 'disabled access' became accepted as a desirable objective wherever exhibitions and new displays were being planned, or when money was available for extending or upgrading existing buildings. There are estimated to be more than 6 million disabled adults in Great Britain – more than 14 per cent of the population (HMSO, 1988: 25). The disabled constitute a significantly large minority within the population, and an important segment of any museum or gallery's potential audience.

While the number of disabled people in Britain is staggeringly large, the population *affected* by disability is even larger. For disabled people, like everyone else, are also the wives, husbands, children, parents and friends of other – 'able' – people. The disabilities of the disabled affect the movement, lives and activities of their able companions. If a person in a wheelchair cannot enter a building, their able-bodied companion is hardly likely to enter either. And if a person with poor sight finds that the lighting, labelling, support information and presentation within a museum or art gallery prevents a response to, and interaction with, the material on display, their fully-sighted companion is hardly likely to propose a museum or gallery visit as a way of their spending time together.

Distinguishing and identifying

'Disablement' is a catch-all word. It covers a very wide range of physical, sensory and learning problems to do with vision, hearing, and mobility. The most frequently used symbol to signify disabled access to a building, or special facilities for the disabled within a building, is, however, the diagrammatic representation of a person in a wheelchair. People in wheelchairs are the most visible and easily understood of those with disabilities. Their problem is (apparently) clear and dramatic. In contrast, the person who is deaf or visually impaired is not immediately obvious. Their disabilities are hidden.

'The disabled', although lumped together under the one word, are not a homogenous group. Different kinds and degrees of disability pose different problems and affect different people in different ways.

A lack of sight is quite different from a lack of hearing, both of which are quite different from an inability to walk. And the effect of a physical or sensory handicap on a 75-year-old can be quite different from the same handicap as experienced by a 12-year-old. Meanwhile, the only thing that a person with sight loss, a person with hearing loss and a person who cannot walk necessarily have in common is that others treat and classify them *as disabled*. They are all marginalized, and may all experience that marginalization in similar ways. That is not a result of their separate disabilities, but is to do with a common societal response to their separate and different needs and problems.

This paper is concerned with just one disability – visual handicap. But even the simple label, 'visual handicap' describes an incredibly wide spectrum of problems, from the minority who have no usable vision whatsoever, to a great variety of people with different kinds and degrees of severe but not total sight loss.

Most museums and galleries assume a certain degree of *good* vision as a prerequisite for the experience that they offer. The art gallery not only assumes the ability to see: its business is to present some of the most developed and sophisticated products of vision. Meanwhile most history, science, folk-life and industrial museums presuppose good eyesight as the normal (and often the only) way to 'read' and interact with their displays. Traditionally it was simply taken for granted that poor eyesight excluded the sufferer from the enjoyment of art galleries and museums – just as it rendered the comprehension of film and live drama difficult, and made many careers and interests open to the sighted person impossible. But in the last twenty years, and in particular over the last decade, a lot of work has been done to begin to open up the experiences offered by art galleries and museums to the visually handicapped. The achievement is limited: it is more often to do with 'one off' events and exhibitions, rather than permanent changes in policy or ways of working. But, nevertheless, more attention is beginning to be paid to the actual and varied nature of vision, and the actual and varied needs, interests and *rights* of the visually handicapped.

Rights and concessions: independence and dependence

It is important to mention rights in this context, because there are, in essence, two extremes in the way that disability issues have been approached.

One extreme is represented by the traditional charitable approach. Within this people of goodwill and those with money make special effort to *help* the disabled. The help is discretionary. It is up to the goodwill and charity of those willing to give time or money. The disabled are provided with special transport – when and where it can be afforded. They are given occasional special holidays, special trips, and special work opportunities. They may be offered special evenings – at a theatre, in a music hall, or at a museum. But in all this the disabled person is *dependent* – waiting upon the time, money and goodwill of others. They have to accept (and be grateful) for what they get. They cannot expect. They do not have rights – they cannot take services, facilities and access for granted – as can an ordinary able-bodied person.

At the other extreme is the argument for *rights* – for the disabled person having, both in law and in practice, the same rights as should every other person. They can expect, they can demand, they can take for granted. They are not dependent. They do not need to rely on special help. They can take for granted an environment and services and systems which *enable* their access and enjoyment and work opportunities to the same or similar degree as every other citizen.

Marcus Weisen, Arts Officer with the Royal National Institute for the Blind, is a strong protagonist for rights. The UK has no tradition of rights. Power passes from crown *down* to parliament: not from people *up* to parliament. Freedoms are granted: not assumed. Not surprisingly, therefore, those who argue for rights often go outside the UK for their models and solutions. In a talk to a European conference on 'Creativity of Disabled People' Marcus Weisen cited the Universal Declaration of Human rights. Article 27.1 states that 'everyone has the right to participate freely in the artistic and cultural life of the community' (Weisen, 1988a: 83). From such a simple declaration many other things should follow. Having rights is about *independence*. It is to do with freedom. But also it is to do with the many practical things that would have to follow – that would have to be done – if such a declaration of rights were to be accepted in practice as well as in theory.

The acceptance of rights would not do away with charity and with the need for individuals to work together for the good of others. But the establishment and acceptance of rights would leave charitable workers free to deal with the special and extraordinary problems and crises in life. Large minorities should not have to live their lives dependent on a daily basis upon the private goodwill and generosity of others simply because they cannot walk, or see, or hear.

In practice, much of the interesting work that is taking place in Britain in developing, building and arguing for access for the disabled falls between the two extremes of charity and rights. And many people who are forced to work from the former position would much prefer (and actively argue for) the latter.

These points are important at the outset of this discussion. The British have a long and respectable tradition of 'good works' for the needy, the poor and the disadvantaged. Much has been achieved within that tradition. It is an important tradition: as a historical study it is a fascinating and inspiring tradition. But today a civilized society should be one that has moved beyond that tradition – where charity is applying itself to new fields, and basic rights for all are established. To quote again Marcus Weisen – this time translating freely from Valéry Giscard d'Estaing: 'You can judge the value of a society by the way it deals with its sick and disabled people' (Weisen, 1988a: 83).

The numbers involved

A recent Office of Population Censuses and Surveys (OPCS) report on the prevalence of disability among adults, estimated that there are 1,668,000 adults in Britain with a visual impairment (HMSO, 1988). This, along with figures for the numbers of people with other disabilities, was far higher than previous official estimates. The OPCS figure for visual impairment is four times the figure for 'registered' blind and partially-sighted adults;[1] 1.68 million adults is a lot of people. Many of them are elderly and have lost sight through illnesses and problems associated with ageing. But roughly a quarter are younger people – 400,000 of them. The kind and degree of visual impairment among this large group of people vary immensely. Very few of them are completely blind. There is a misconception that 'blind' people have no sight. In fact, most people with visual impairments, including the majority of those whose loss is severe enough to be registerable as 'blind', have some usable sight. For the most severely handicapped this may be no more than the perception of light and dark. But for many blind people their residual vision is usable – given the right circumstances or aids.[2]

A person is registerable as partially-sighted when their sight is so poor that they have to be eighteen feet away from something in order to see it with the same 'clarity' as a fully-sighted person. They are registerable as blind if the distance has to be reduced to nine feet. Thus, where a fully-sighted person may be able to read the writing on a sign or advertisement hoarding from 180 feet or more away, the blind person has to be standing nine feet away, or less.[3]

I used the word 'clarity' above. That is, of course, misleading, because the way in which the visually impaired person sees varies with different conditions. A person with tunnel vision may see very clearly, but their field of vision is very restricted. In contrast, many people have problems resulting from a loss of central vision. They can see something throughout the visual field, but their greatest loss of clarity and detail is in the central areas – the very areas where the 'normal' eye provides most in terms of detail and clarity. Others again have vision that is patchy involving different kinds of loss or blurredness or blockage in different parts of the visual field. Others again suffer interference in their vision in the form of flashing light. The variations in what can go wrong and how this can affect or limit sight are legion.[4]

No one expects the world at large, let alone those in charge of museums and galleries, to acquire a detailed knowledge of the many differing kinds of sight loss. Two important points should be recognized, however: first, that the majority of visually handicapped people, including the majority of those registerable as blind, do have some *usable* vision: second, that the nature (the effect) of different kinds of sight impairment is very varied. One of the breakthroughs of recent years has been the recognition that all sight is usable. The person with limited vision can still see. They have a sight that they use and which, with a little help, they can use to greater effect.

Touch and vision; the normal and the special

The recognition that the majority of visually handicapped people have some sight has been important in affecting the range and kind of work that museums and galleries have developed with, and for, blind and partially sighted people.

Exhibitions within which some or all of the objects on display can be *touched* are the most obvious kind of provision for those with severe visual handicaps. The idea of touch exhibitions developed in the United States, but the late 1980s in Britain saw a remarkable growth in interest. In December 1988 reference was made to more than fifteen British art galleries having staged touch exhibitions within the previous two years (Weisen, 1988b). Since then the monthly 'Art to Share' column of the magazine *New Beacon*[5] has carried a regular listing of special exhibitions, touch sessions and events around the country.

Although touch exhibitions are now sufficiently common to provide material for a regular monthly listing in a specialist magazine, they are still enough of a rarity that they constitute a curiosity wherever they are held. But at the same time they are sufficient in number for experience and understanding to be grow-ing–at least for those with a professional involvement in their organization and assessment (Raffrey, 1988). In particular organizers are learning what can and cannot be achieved through touch, and what touch is. Among the important lessons learned, has been that touch is not a simple substitute for seeing. As artist Jefford Horrigan wrote in a report on touch workshops held at the Whitechapel Art Gallery:

> It is a myth perpetuated by Hollywood, that the blind and partially sighted touch the faces of others in order to find out what they look like. For many, asking permission, or even having the desire to touch another's face, is unthinkable, even if they are the faces of people they are close to. It is the voice, its tone and inflections which are the guide to age, sex, temperament and personality. Sighted people must be careful not to impose their own values and to consider touch as an imitation or substitute for looking in another form (Horrigan, 1988: 2).

While it is important not to see touch as a substitute for sight, it is equally important to recognize that touch can be a way of under-standing and responding in its own right. It should be much more than a way of gathering simple information. Marcus Weisen goes so far as to suggest that touch may have an aesthetic of its own (1986).[6] Blind arts consultant, William Kirby, concentrates in his work more on the use of touch in *combination with* using residual vision. As a warning against both ignoring residual vision and imposing false limitations on touch, he recounts an experience of visiting a touch exhibition early on in his new career as a blind arts consultant:

> After I had a series of enlightening experiences which led me to my present

work, I proudly took my white symbol cane and my registration card to a national exhibition exclusively for 'the Blind'. When I suggested that the spotlighting of a piece of sculpture would have made its craggy head and shoulders more visible, my kind voluntary guide told me: 'You are not supposed to be able to see anything'. So I decided to play the game and close my eyes. I was guided to another piece to identify. When my hands recognised it as a dog I was congratulated and invited to move on. I was not told that Elizabeth Frink was saying something special about dogs, nor was it suggested that I might look for more tactile clues about her intentions (Kirby, 1988b).

Kirby's story makes three points. First, that touch is not simply about recognition: it must also be about understanding. Second, that for understanding to be meaningful the toucher needs to be given other contextualizing information to work with – just as an ordinary sighted viewer would need or benefit from the same. And, third, that his residual vision should not have been denied. His suggestion about the possible use of spotlighting was constructive and important: it was about a way of maximizing the visibility of the work for those with little vision.

From touch exhibitions for the handicapped have developed other exhibitions presented as being for the visually impaired *and* the fully-sighted to share. Touch is a much neglected sense. Much sculpture is made by hand – is touched, manipulated, cut, polished and in other ways made *with the hands*. Touch can, therefore, be an important extension to its appreciation – for the fully-sighted as well as for the less sighted. The development of exhibitions that are designed to work both for the blind and for those with partial and full sight is also important because it is a move towards 'normalization'. Normalization is about integration – about maximizing access on a routine basis. It is to do with creating the possibility for independence – independent visiting, and enjoyment, of museums and galleries for the visually impaired and the disabled in general. Segregated special events are the opposite of normalization. They were important as learning experiences. They provided understanding that could lead on to integrated events – to an experience that was for sharing.

Important in moving towards greater access for all is picking up on Kirby's suggestion above for spotlighting on a particular piece of work. Kirby was asking to be able to use his vision. He was, in effect, locating himself at a particular point along a spectrum from total blindness to total sight. The registerable blind and partially sighted cluster towards one end of that spectrum. The majority of the young tend towards the other end of the spectrum. Many other people fall somewhere in-between. An integrated approach to presenting material allows maximum access for the widest range of people to all 'normal', displays, while also providing those extras in terms of commentary, information, facilities and help that will enable those with the severest loss of hearing, sight, or mobility to respond to, and gain from, what is offered.

This is not to reject the validity of some special exhibitions which are put on specially or exclusively for the blind. At the end of this essay reference is made, for example, to a successful exhibition in Belgium put on to interpret cathedral architecture to those with no vision (Van Alphen, 1983). That was not an exhibition *for all*. It was an exhibition very specifically communicating information about and the experience of the space and construction and aesthetics of a building to people who, though knowing and using the building, could not see and experience its design and dimensions, or the builder's intentions. And I have myself been involved in organizing publicity for an exhibition in Wales of 'raised' oil paintings.[7] Although the show was open to all, the painter had specifically made the works for the blind, in order to make possible a discussion about the nature of seeing. The show was aimed at the blind and was about sight. As such it worked as a *special* show.

There is always room for such 'special' exhibitions. There are special exhibitions of all kinds targeted at very specific audiences. The point about integration, however, is that overall, and when dealing with 'ordinary' or mainstream exhibitions and displays, the aim of integration is to provide maximum access for all on a regular basis. To allow the disabled to participate as fully as possible in the work of museums and galleries as people – not just on an occasional and concessionary basis as 'the disabled'.

Sight, seeing and art

Visual handicap has a special interest in relation to art exhibitions and art museums, because the handicap relates to the very act of seeing itself. The handicap is not simply to do with arriving at, getting into or moving around within the place where the exhibition is being presented. The handicap is itself central to the *experience* of that which is presented. Or at least so it would seem. The nature of sight needs much further consideration – more than there is space for here. But certainly it is clear that it would be facile, for example, to assume that a visual aesthetic experience – the experience, say, of a particular painting – is at its maximum for those with 20/20 vision, and diminishes accordingly as vision moves towards total blindness. Vision is not like that; aesthetic experience is not like that.

Seeing is both an interactive and a used thing. It is to do with expectations, knowledge, recognition, and the way people use their eyes in 'reading' that which is before them and around them. Seeing seems a simple act. It is, in fact, incredibly complex. And how people use and develop their sight can vary greatly (see, for example, Pratt, 1990). Appropriate examples of how limited sight does not necessarily prevent developed vision are provided by Patrick Trevor-Roper in his book, *The World through Blunted Sight* (1988). The evidence he presents for the kinds and degrees of limited vision experienced by many well-known artists is fascinating. The quality of information available on the problems of artists from past centuries is often limited. But the acute problems in seeing experienced by Degas throughout most of his working life are clear. And Cézanne is recorded not only as being myopic (and refusing to wear corrective glasses) but also to have possibly suffered some retinal damage due to diabetes. Trevor-Roper quotes Huysmans' assessment of Cézanne as: 'An artist with a diseased retina, who, exasperated by a defective vision, discovered the basis of a new art' (1988: 37). Trevor-Roper's examples are all historical. In the last few years there have also been a number of interesting art exhibitions incorporating sculpture and painting by contemporary visually handicapped artists – artists who have been through art college, and who are seeking to practise as professional artists.[8]

It is brave for a visually handicapped artist to put work into such a show. For the last thing that most artists want to be known for is their handicap. As with all successful artists who have had impaired vision, they want to be known for their work.

Normality and...

In the past, of course, many artists – perhaps most – would have had to accept a fairly severe loss of vision at some point in their lives.

Corrective lenses have not always been readily available to deal with the otherwise severe sight loss that can result from having short or long sight. Today people with severe visual impairment are unusual. They are a minority within the general population. But before the mass availability of good quality corrective lenses for people with short and long sight those with other visual handicaps would simply have been suffering from different and/or more severe degrees of a common problem. Trevor-Roper, whose speculations on the personality implications of short and long sight are interesting if not always entirely convincing, points out that until this century spectacles 'were a luxury, normally chosen by trial and error from an itinerant vendor's tray, and frowned on by most nineteenth century occulists, who held them to be damaging to the eyes' (1988: 17).

In Europe 15–20 per cent of the population suffers from myopia, that is are short sighted, and would have very poor distance vision without corrective lenses. In China and Japan the figure is as high as 60–70 per cent. And in Europe about 50 per cent of the population is hypermetropic, that is, are long sighted, and need corrective lenses for close vision (Trevor-Roper, 1988: 20). These figures are of little consequence today. Providing not only corrective lenses but spectacles as a fashion accessory is a major industry. But just try and imagine a world a century or more ago when glasses were much less common, or were only available to the rich, if at all: a world in which the 'normal' deterioration in close vision that often comes with age was not corrected: and in which the 'blurred' vision that so many people only experience when they take their glasses off was their only vision.

We are used to asking children to imagine a time before cars, without electricity, before instant heating, and when most people started work at the age of twelve or less. It is a useful exercise to encourage children to think about and imagine the past. But it can be interesting for adults, too, looking around a museum of art to speculate on what it means that most of the paintings, sculpture, fine furniture and other objects which we prize from the past come from an age when poor sight must have been normal – or at least when making the best that you could of the vision that you had was a reality for a sizeable proportion of the population.[9]

An exercise in sensitizing

I first became involved in issues to do with art and disability when working during the 1980s in the Art Department of the Welsh Arts Council. I was aware of the occasional reference to touch exhibitions in the art press. I had been approached for administrative help and marketing advice by an artist who was working on an exhibition of 'raised' paintings – paintings designed to be read by touch as well as seen by the eye. I knew that a man in Winchester had set up as a specialist consultant on matters to do with art and visual disability. And I was beginning to confront the nature of my own poor sight – a problem that to some extent I had overcome through avoiding it for the previous thirty or so years. The projects I became involved with through the Welsh Arts Council included:

1988   commissioning visually handicapped arts consultant William Kirby to make visits to and prepare detailed reports on and for twelve galleries and museums in Wales on how they could improve their facilities and services for the visually handicapped;

1989   organizing a conference about vision, visual handicap and the visual arts. Called 'Creative Seeing' this brought together museum and gallery staff (including many of those visited by William Kirby), social workers, artists, teachers, and the visually handicapped. Speakers included Marcus Weisen, Arts Officer with the Royal National Institute for the Blind; Rosanna Nicholson, Assistant Curator at the Gunnersbury Park Museum in London (host to a recent exhibition of work by visually handicapped artists); John Everett, a sculptor and teacher at the Royal National College for the Blind in Hereford; Gaynor Edwards, an artist working on exhibitions specially produced for the blind; and William Kirby, the arts consultant who had prepared the reports on the galleries and museums;

1987–9 advising and organizing publicity for artist Gaynor Edwards in preparing and presenting a special exhibition of sculpture and raised paintings designed specifically for the blind and partially sighted and exhibited at venues in Swansea, Cwmbran and Llanbedrog (near Pwllheli);

1986–9 featuring and publicizing all the above and other events to

do with art and the visually handicapped in the Welsh Arts
Council's quarterly visual arts magazine, *Art News*.

All of the above were intended to explore and develop a wider
awareness of both the needs of the visually handicapped, and ways of
meeting those needs. The visits by William Kirby to twelve of the key
galleries and museums in Wales were of particular importance in
being an attempt to develop understanding through direct face-to-
face contact and discussion followed up by a report.

The museums and galleries visited by Kirby embraced a wide range
of types of venue.

1.   In the south east – *Newport Museum and Art Gallery*: a local
authority museum and art gallery where library, museum and art
gallery share a building above a modern shopping centre, the art
gallery having both a permanent collection and a strong programme
of temporary exhibitions; *Llantarnam Grange Arts Centre in
Cwmbran*: an independent arts centre with arts council, regional arts
association and other funding; *Chapter Arts Centre, Cardiff*: an
independent multi-purpose arts centre with arts council and local
authority funding, having several exhibition areas, a theatre, cinemas,
restaurant, and workshops; *St David's Hall, Cardiff*: an international
concert hall with art exhibitions held in the level two foyer area.
2.   In the south and west – *The Glynn Vivian Art Gallery and
Museum, Swansea*: a local authority museum and art gallery combining a permanent art collection, a porcelain collection, and a modern
temporary exhibition gallery; *Carmarthen Museum*: a local authority
local history museum in a former palace of the Bishop of St Davids,
with a mixed museum collection and a temporary exhibition area.
3.   In mid-Wales – *Aberystwyth Arts Centre*: a multi-function arts
centre on the university campus with an important ceramic collection,
theatre space and two principal exhibition areas, with funding from
the arts council and others; *Oriel 31, Newton*: an independent art
gallery with arts council funding and a mixed programme of
temporary exhibitions.
4.   In north Wales – *Wrexham Arts Centre*: an exhibition room and
other arts activities within a local authority library building; *The
Mostyn Art Gallery, Llandudno*: an independent art gallery with arts
council funding, a changing programme of temporary exhibitions
and a specialist crafts area; *The Tegfryn Art Gallery, Menai Bridge*:
one of the longer established private galleries in North Wales having

mixed displays, special temporary exhibitions and tending to work with a stable of artists; *Plas Glyn y Weddw Art Gallery, Llanbedrog, near Pwellhli*: a large private gallery in a mid-nineteenth-century mock Gothic mansion mounting a programme of temporary exhibitions in some spaces and having mixed displays in other rooms. Ceramics and small sculpture also displayed.

In each venue visited Kirby met and was shown round the premises by a member of staff, with whom he discussed both the gallery or museum's existing facilities, and the kinds of developments that were then taking place in terms of not only special exhibitions for the visually handicapped, but, more importantly, improvements in presentation, information provision, and access that would generally improve galleries and museums both for people with visual handicaps and for the population in general. The visits were followed up with a substantial written report that assessed the venue's existing facilities, made suggestions for improvement, and contained further information about current developments elsewhere.

My impression of the reaction from galleries and museums to the idea of Kirby's visits was a mixture of curiosity, guilt, a serious wish to learn, and in some cases real enthusiasm to take things forward. Personally, I believed that the whole project was important and worthwhile, but I was pessimistic at the time about its likely achievement. Even with the follow-up conference in February 1989, one of the purposes of which was to keep the issue live and re-focus attention on the questions Kirby had raised, I expected the whole venture to engender a lot of good intentions, but little long-term action.

The visits certainly aroused great interest, and in particular at venues such as those at Carmarthen and Aberystwyth, where there had been some previous involvement with the visually impaired. All listened with careful attention to the things Kirby said. And the subsequent reports were full and detailed. In May 1990, therefore, no longer working for the Welsh Arts Council, I circulated a questionnaire and letter to the twelve galleries and museums who had been part of the project, seeking some basic information on what, if anything, had been done as a result of the visits, reports and conference. The galleries and museums in Newport, Cwmbran, Cardiff, Carmarthen, Aberystwyth, Llandudno and Llanbedrog replied – eight out of the twelve. Overall the content of the eight responses was more positive than I had expected.

I asked thirteen questions concerning whether or not the galleries had or had not done various things *specifically following and as a result of* William Kirby's visit to, and report for, the museum or gallery. To six of the thirteen questions three or more of the eight galleries who replied gave positive answers: three had encouraged the touching of some objects; three had increased or altered lighting so as to increase contrast or, in other ways, enhance the visibility of some objects; three had moved captions or written information forward within display cases so as to increase legibility; two described this question as not applicable – presumably because they did not use display cases; four had increased the print size of captions/labels adjacent to objects or paintings; three had increased the density of print on labels and captions or in other ways enhanced the contrast between writing and background; and three had re-positioned captions or labels on walls so as to be at eye level; a fourth said that they had done this anyway before Kirby's visit.

While these are all only small steps, encouragingly the improvements were not all concentrated amongst the same three or four galleries. Six of the eight had taken some steps to improve access and presentation for the visually handicapped following Kirby's visit. In one of the six the member of staff most involved with the issue had also prepared a detailed report with a number of important and clear recommendations which, if followed through, would have initiated major improvements to the environment for all visitors with less than perfect sight. Finally in the two cases where nothing had been done a covering note indicated that it was hoped to introduce improved access for the disabled in general when staffing and resources permitted.

There were negative answers to seven of the questions I asked: no venue had introduced large print guides or leaflets; none had introduced any information in moon or braille; none had altered the interior environment to make mobility easier for the visually impaired – by, for example, altering decor, lighting, wall and floor coverings, or contrast at step edges. However one gallery commented that mobility was already fairly adequate in their gallery, being flat and on ground floor; none had repositioned or replaced directional signs, door signs and room or exhibition identification signs so as to make them more legible for the visually handicapped; none had prepared leaflets, information or mailshots, targeted specifically at attracting more disabled visitors or, in particular, more visually handicapped visitors; one venue said that they 'sometimes' used taped/casette guides to exhibits, particular displays or special exhibitions.

There is a lot, therefore, that had not happened.[10] The visits, reports, conference and the periodic articles in the magazine *Art News* (which all the galleries received) had helped build up awareness, understanding and goodwill: and small advances had been made. Perhaps the most revealing of the answers above is that no gallery or museum had (or had been able to) prepare leaflets, information or mailshots targeted specifically at attracting more disabled or more visually impaired visitors. They neither had, nor had sought to, establish any kind of ongoing relationship with the visually handicapped community. Therein lies part of the problem.

Unless the disabled are sought out and *invited*, they will not come to have any reason to suppose that they will be welcomed, or that they will be able to gain access to or make any sense of what is in a museum or gallery. At the same time there is little point in making special effort to identify, target and involve the disabled (or any special category of disabled person), unless you have some facilities and resources (technical or personnel) with which to respond when they come. There needs to be a two-pronged approach: the development of facilities, in tandem with identifying and bringing in the target audience. People will not just come 'on spec': they will have had too many years of experiencing the impossibility of a visit to a museum or gallery. But if efforts are made to invite and involve, then the facilities must be there when they arrive.

I am not despondent about the results from the initiatives that the Welsh Arts Council took with William Kirby in Wales. Half of the galleries and museums visited reported some improvement as a result of the initiative. Two thirds showed interest in taking matters further. All of them have the usual problems of staffing levels, time, money, and so on. For each gallery and museum separately it is difficult to take developments as far forward as they might wish. The initiative in Wales was a modest one, but it was the first effort of its kind in any part of the UK to try a coordinated approach to raising the issues and problems faced by the visually impaired, combining individual reports and personal visits with a conference and the general distribution of information.

The response thus far shows that if such an initiative were followed through over a longer time period better results could be achieved. It is also important that such developments should become part of mainstream arts funding and policymaking, and not hived off into the interesting but quiet side-waters of 'disability funding'. At the Welsh Arts Council, although I was employed within the Art Department, the work with William Kirby was part of a separately funded initiative to do with disability issues, and involved no policy commitment or long-term development work on the part of the Art Department. The conference was self-financing.

Confirmation of limitations

William Kirby's visits in Wales indicated a level of interest, but also the reality of how little was being done. On a wider British level in 1988 the Royal National Institute for the Blind, in cooperation with the Museums Association's Database, organized a survey of 2,400 museums. Questionnaires were distributed, and 1,400 responded. The purpose of the survey was to gather some basic general information about the real extent of the work being done with and for the visually impaired in museums across Britain.

Encouragingly, 312 of those who responded (22.28 per cent) reported having received groups of visually impaired adults during the two-year period prior to the survey. Even more encouragingly, 600 of those who replied (42.86 per cent) reported making at least ten items available for touching – although the majority had no guide available to help the visitor. In general, however, the results of the survey were sobering (see Kirby and Weisen, 1989; Weisen, 1990). Only 2.5 per cent of the respondents could provide a braille guide. 4.5 per cent had a cassette guide – but not necessarily designed to guide the visually impaired visitor. 3.9 per cent had a large print guide. 6.9 per cent have permanent lighting which might enhance the use of low vision. And 9.9 per cent report providing large print labels.

The picture was not altogether gloomy. Something was being achieved in some places. But it was very little and spread very thinly. The results of the survey offered a strong dose of realism to counter the optimism of those specialists and enthusiasts who, spending much of their time helping to organize and promote touch exhibitions and special events for the visually impaired, might have failed to notice how limited and occasional real provision and development was across the country. Summarizing the most pessimistic aspect of the survey results Marcus Weisen concluded in a report that:

Museums which make an independent visit by visually impaired people (as opposed to pre-arranged guided tours) possible and attractive are largely non-existent. Where these facilities exist, they are not, in most cases advertised in information leaflets or guidebooks, and even less so in accessible form (1990: 15).

Interpretation and information

I have referred at a number of points in this article to the importance of information, while stressing concepts such as 'independence' and 'normality'. In essence I would argue that the goal of any serious policy towards the visually handicapped, as towards any sector of the disabled, is to create a situation where they can visit museums and galleries independently, and they can do so in as 'normal' a way as possible. The Royal National Institute for the Blind's survey (above) indicates how little such normal and independent visiting is currently possible.

I have also talked of those with severe visual impairment as being at one end of a spectrum between the two ends of which fall a large part of the population. Clarity and conciseness of labelling, bringing information forward rather than keeping it to the rear, providing various kinds and size of print, providing information on tape, leaflets, handouts, information sheets and other forms of commentary, and giving more thought to the layout of buildings and the information available about building layout, are all things that will benefit both the severely visually impaired, and the moderately visually impaired, as well as the 'ordinary' visitor. Many museums would agree that, with time and resources, there is much that they could do to improve the quality and range of the support information they provide to their displays. Much of such improvement can be designed so as to benefit disabled and able-bodied alike.

Because very often the problems of the disabled are no more than acute versions of the problems encountered by many able-bodied museum visitors. 'Special' events and exhibitions targeted at the disabled can be stimulating – can build experience and will introduce many people to new experiences for the first time. But in the long term what is needed is normalization. That is to say, access, interpretation and information such as will allow the disabled independent access to a museum's permanent and 'ordinary' exhibits.

An interesting development in opening up an art museum's permanent collection to the visually impaired has been started by the

Living Paintings Trust.[11] The Trust is developing special information packs to help the visually impaired in seeing selected major works in some of the country's larger collections. Each pack deals with ten images, and includes: a raised, tactile, thermoform version of the image; a taped commentary on the image; a postcard sized reproduction of the image; a typed version of the tape commentary. The pack and its various kinds of information follows from the understanding that seeing is based on knowledge. The brain does not simply receive the mass of visual information received through the eye and optic nerve: it makes sense of it and 'reads' and constructs it according to experience and knowledge.

Only in near-darkness or when looking at the far distance will the fully-sighted person have the experience of trying to 'work out' what something may be, with that sudden flash of recognition and clarity that comes when you realize what it is, and immediately the thing seen 'becomes obvious'. For a person with severe visual impairment viewing a large oil painting from a distance of six or seven feet in a museum may pose similar problems. The Living Paintings Trust's raised tactile version of the image, therefore, provides them with a structure to feel and thus to inform their looking. The taped commentary similarly guides them around and through the image. The intention is that the two together will enable the viewer to suddenly 'make sense' of what they see. Something which they could only part see and only hesitantly decode suddenly 'becomes obvious'.

The work of the Trust has produced a very mixed response, ranging from strong enthusiasm to severe doubts.[12] Many who have been blind from birth find the exercise to have little meaning. The experience of seeing cannot be conveyed by a tactile diagram. For others who have gone blind later in life the combination of tape and tactile image has provided an interesting and sometimes exciting stimulus to memory.[13] And for some who, although having suffered severe sight loss, still retain some vision, the Trust's packs have worked precisely as intended. Gioya Steinke falls into this latter category. She is quoted as saying:

> I have been able to visit galleries with a renewed zeal and fresh confidence; and can participate in many of the famous pictures that were merely a blur to me before. I am able to see strong colours and some shapes and curves and these can now be assembled into a picture in the mind's eye. Often I can actually see with my damaged vision, if colour, form and subject are pointed out.[14]

I believe that Gioya Steinke is precisely the kind of person for whom one would expect the Living Paintings Trust's approach to work. The packs are an *aid to* seeing: not a *substitute for* seeing. Given that the majority of visually impaired people have some usable sight, I think that the usefulness of the Trust's approach is largely in providing an important service to such people. Among those reported[15] as now working with the Living Paintings Trust on introducing packs for their collections are the Tate Gallery in London and the Burrell Collection in Glasgow.

Another interesting approach to interpreting material for the visually impaired is provided by the Cathedrals Through Touch and Hearing project. The project, directed by Professor John Hull and based at the Centre for Religious Education Development and Research of Birmingham University, seeks to develop new ways of enabling blind and partially sighted people to respond to religious architecture. A wooden scale model, ground plan, braille and large print literature, and cassette commentary and acoustic guide are provided to enable the blind and visually impaired to relate to and understand the cathedral as they move through it. The largest interpretive display is at Gloucester Cathedral, with small centres at Lichfield, Coventry, Worcester, Hereford and Birmingham cathedrals.[16]

An innovative exhibition presenting the Gothic cathedral to the blind visitor was organized at the Royal Museum of Art and History in Brussels in 1982 (Van Alphen, 1983). The museum, which at the time already had eleven years experience of developing exhibitions for the visually impaired, presented an exhibition which combined models, raised plans and taped cassette information with original tools, gargoyles, figures, and examples of vaulting. The exhibition aimed to be didactic as well as aesthetic. Models of Gothic windows were constructed so that the development of the tracery could be followed through. Models of the development of the medieval town were made so that the growth of the cathedral could be observed. All this was supported by lectures and, for the blind, a special visit to the cathedral upon which much of the exhibition was based.

The exhibition, like others at the Royal Museum of Art and History, ran for eight months. The accounts of it suggest a museum which had put a decade of experience to good use in thinking through in advance how to convey information and experience in a non-visual way, and how to bring to life an understanding of real buildings in a way which the blind could enter into.

The Royal Museum of Art and History's exhibition was dealing with an everyday phenomenon – the church or cathedral – but presenting it in such a way that it could be understood by a very particular audience – those with little or no vision. That requires careful thought. The exhibition maker needs to put him or herself in the position of the visually impaired person. The aim of the exhibition for the visually impaired is the same as the aim is or would be for the sighted person – that the visitor achieves a heightened understanding and appreciation of the subject. But the mode of interpretation, and the ordering and presentation of support information and contextualizing detail and the ways in which information is conveyed may need to be different. Not always *that* different; just a bit different. Besides, as is so often repeated, the things that make an exhibition or display more accessible for the visually impaired person are often the very same things that make exhibitions and displays more accessible to the public at large.

Conclusion – permanence and rights

In this paper I have touched briefly on some of the issues to do with vision, art, museums and the visually impaired. It is a field where a great deal has happened, and a great deal has been learned. But, like so much that is to do with the disabled, it is also a field where there is much enthusiasm and many moments of special effort, but little long-term achievement: little 'normalization'. Here I have sought to go beyond dealing just with sight in terms of disablement, to raise questions to do with the nature of sight, the variations in sight, the interactive and learned nature of seeing, and the recentness of 'normal' sight being general *good* sight. Through such discussion I have tried to open up the understanding of what sight is, what it is to have impaired sight, and how important different kinds of information and guidance are to *enable* and make possible the sight and seeing of those with limited but usable vision. I have also described projects I have been involved with in Wales – projects aimed at raising awareness of what sight is, and what museums and galleries could do. The work was a beginning. Like much other work, it showed what could be done, and where things could go.

My own involvement with projects in Wales also made clear to me the impossibility of any real long-term and solid achievement without strong leadership at the policymaking level. It is not enough that individuals within some museums, and individual museums within some areas try and do the occasional special exhibition, or make modest improvements to layout, presentation or support information. The real breakthrough for the visually impaired, as for all disabled people, comes only when the things that make access, understanding and enjoyment for the visually impaired at all museums become *normal*. Only then can one talk about the disabled having access – when access is a *right* – but a right that is so commonplace that it is simply normal. Only then will disability and museums cease to be an issue. That must be the aim – 'issues' only exist when things are not right – when things cannot be done, or cannot be done well. If the aim is integration and normalization, that will take acceptance and action at a policymaking level. Action by arts councils, area museum councils, local authorities and other similar bodies will help. But ultimately action has to be taken at government level – in Britain or in Europe. Only then will the necessary expenditure, planning and care become routine – become normal.

Normalization may seem – probably is – a long way off. But more and more debate takes place and pressure is applied at international levels. In Britain the European dimension becomes increasingly important. It is at that level that experience is shared, and where perhaps hope lies for the establishment of *rights*, as opposed to *concessions*.[17]

Notes

1. Registration as blind or partially-sighted is not automatic. The individual can choose whether or not to be registered.
2. According to William Kirby (1988a), 4 per cent of visually impaired people are totally blind, and 85 per cent 'have some useful vision'.
3. Other issues may also be taken into account, including inability to do a job for which sight is considered necessary. For a discussion of the registration process, see 'The New BD8', *New Beacon*, April 1990.
4. See the leaflet, *Partial Sight*, available from the Partially Sighted Society, Queens Road, Doncaster DN1 2NX.
5. *New Beacon*, published monthly by the Royal National Institute for the Blind, 224 Great Portland Street, London.
6. See also Marcus Weisen, 'Beauty is in the eye of the Beholder?', letter in the *British Journal of Visual Impairment*, Summer 1988.

7. Gaynor Edwards, 'Painting and Sculpture to Touch', shown between 1987 and 1989 in venues in Swansea, Cwmbran and Llanbedrog (Pwllheli).
8. For example, 'An Eye for Art', held at the Gunnersbury Park Museum, London 1988. See Ailsa Turner's report on the exhibition in *New Beacon*, November 1988.
9. Spectacles of some sort have been known since at least the thirteenth century. However, large-scale manufacture of good quality lenses in light weight frames did not start in Britain till the early nineteenth century.
10. I have quoted thirteen specific questions to do with possible improvements. Other questions dealt with general disability issues, and space was allowed for respondents to detail any other things they may have done or set up for or with the disabled or the visually impaired.
11. See *Art News* 23, April 1989: 13, published by the Welsh Arts Council, Cardiff, and the *Brtitish Journal of Visual Impairment*, Spring 1990: 24.
12. See *British Journal of Visual Impairment*, Spring 1990: 24.
13. The distinction between those totally blind from birth, and those who have lost sight later in life, is important when considering the presentation of certain kinds of sculptural, three dimensional and diagramatic material to the blind. See, for example, the comment in the penultimate paragraph of 'Tate Gallery Sculpture Exhibition for the Blind and Partially Sighted', *Inter Regional Review*, Winter 1981/82.
14. See *British Journal of Visual Impairment*, Spring 1990.
15. See *British Journal of Visual Impairment*, Spring 1990.
16. See *British Journal of Visual Impairment*, Spring 1990.
17. See, for example, reports of the August 1990 international conference in Glasgow on *Access to Art and Cultural Heritage*. Organized by the Royal National Institute for the Blind on behalf of the European Blind Union, and subtitled 'Visually impaired europeans deserve a better deal in the arts'. Resolutions from the conference were sent to European ministers of arts and culture, and to arts organizations in Europe. The wide-ranging resolutions are notable in being built from principles and declarations of rights. See *Viewpoint*, October 1990, pp. 65–8, published by the National Federation of the Blind.

Bibliography

HMSO, *The Prevalence of Disability among Adults*, Office of Population Census and Surveys (HMSO: London, 1988).

Horrigan, J., 'Jacob Epstein exhibition: report on touch workshops', *British Journal of Visual Impairment*, Spring 1988: 22.

Kirby, W., 'The education of a blind art consultant', *New Beacon* May 1988a: 145.

Kirby, W., 'The art of confronting problems' *New Beacon*, June 1988b: 178.

Kirby, W. and Weisen, M., 'Museums, galleries and the visually impaired', *Museum News* 45, 1989: 2-3.

Pratt, F., 'I simply draw what I see', *The Artist*, September 1990: 28-31.

Raffrey, M., 'The arts through touch perception: present trends and future prospects', *British Journal of Visual Impairment*, Summer 1988: 63-65.

Trevor-Roper, P., *The World Through Blunted Sight* (Penguin: London, 1988).

Van Alphen, J., 'Handling a cathedral', *British Journal of Visual Impairment*, Summer 1983: 2-4.

Weisen, M., 'Cultural integration and creativity of visually handicapped people – towards a european policy', *New Beacon*, February 1988: 47-9; March 1988a: 83-5.

Weisen, M., 'Art in touch', *Artists Newsletter*, December 1988b: 29-31.

Weisen, M., 'The unbearable lightness of politics or the art of inertia', *New Beacon*, April 1990: 135-7.

4

Planning for visitors

GUY WILSON

Introduction

There are not many things about which everyone in the museum
profession agrees, and this is more a sign of the health than of the
sickness of the museum world, but I suspect that few would disagree
that a museum is not a museum if it does not allow people to have
access to its collections in some way or another. There are many
degrees and many forms of public access to museums, and each
institution allows greater or lesser access at various times to its
collections, but if a collection remains forever inaccessible, however
well it is administered and kept, that collection would not be called a
museum by many of us.

It has always seemed to me to be curious, therefore, that despite
this all but universal agreement – that a museum must have a public to
be a museum – so many museum professionals see the public as
enemy number one, their very presence often inimical to all that they
hold dear, and disruptive of all the proper work that they should be
doing. In the 1980s there has been a wide debate about such issues,
and a polarization of views, which I shall discuss shortly. I do not
believe it is an exaggeration, however, to suggest that the fear and
concern experienced by many long-serving members of the museum
profession about the apparently growing demands of the public has
not made easier the task of properly planning for the various visiting
publics which a museum must serve.

This paper is a very personal and a very general survey of where we
are today. It attempts to give no definitive answer, for there is none. It
tries to stimulate thought and discussion of an area of the work of
museums which has been strangely neglected. Too often in the past,
planning for visitors has been haphazard and taken for granted.
Many museums have hierarchical organizational structures very ill-
suited to planning properly for the needs of visitors, which have
grown up largely as a result of the belief that omnipotent, omniscient

curators would rule benignly for the benefit of all. Sadly, life even within museums is far more complex than that, and in recent years there have been awakenings to this around the world – rude or enlightened, depending on your point of view – which have led to a number of painful restructurings in this country and abroad, and an increasingly vociferous and strident debate about the role of the various different professionals who are all required to make a museum function. The 'needs of the visitor' have become something of a pawn and a shibboleth in this debate, and this in itself has not always helped museums properly to plan for the legitimate aspirations of their visitors. None of this is intended to suggest that from the visitors' point of view the vast majority of museums have not changed enormously for the better in the last two decades, for they have. It is, however, intended to justify the need for a survey of attitudes to the needs of visitors and how we plan for them, which I hope will play some small part in more positive approaches to this complex subject in future.

Museums versus the public

If we are honest, I do not think there are many of us in the museum profession who have not at some time resented the effect which the public is having on us or our museum. For example, however public enquiries are dealt with in a museum, there is always the member of the public who seeks to ask us the wrong question at the wrong time, and we resent it. We fulminate internally and unfortunately some-times verbally about people not understanding what museums are for, and not realizing that our time is valuable and that we have much else of greater importance to think of and do right now. For most of us that happens rarely and we feel guilty about it both at the time and afterwards, for we know deep down that we are there to serve that visitor, who is often helping to pay our salaries and maintain the collection which we love. These feelings are inevitable, however, in museum professionals under pressure as almost all are, who see their institutions cracking under the strain of underfunding and under-staffing, yet bursting at the seams with ideas, most of which are destined for the dusty filing cabinet of dreams in which development plans fade and yellow, while the very enthusiasm which gave birth to them is jaundiced by rejection and neglect. When professionals are overworked and under pressure it is understandable that they sometimes over-react to the increasing demands and pressures of the people they serve. However, understanding this does not mean condoning it.

Nor should it hide from us that for some of our colleagues what is for most of us an occasional aberration is almost a religion. I know of some in the profession who at best only pay lip-service to the concept of public service. For these people the collections they work with are theirs to protect and preserve from all comers. The public represents a threat not only to the scholastic quiet required for the completion of pieces of research, sometimes personally lucrative, sometimes worthy but obscure, but also to the very continued existence of the collections which they so sincerely, if selfishly, love.

If this picture is exaggerated, it is, none the less, not inaccurate. These attitudes too, are entirely understandable, and stem from very proper professional concerns. Research and scholastic excellence are vital to all museums and especially to national ones with specialist collections of international importance. Scholars in these museums need time and room and money to pursue their researches if the fundamental educational and academic purposes of museums are to be properly fulfilled. The 1988 report of the Museums and Galleries Commission on national museums was entirely right when it stated:

> It is ... true to say that the intellectual activities of national museums are central to their other purposes. They were founded essentially as institutions for education and research. ... They seek to sustain their collections, and to promote the learning based upon them, so as to serve scholars worldwide. For well over 200 years this concept has attracted men and women of high quality into the service of national museums, informed their thinking and dictated their attitudes. These collections are part of the history of ideas, their curators a species of historian. Their scholarship must be of a quality that commands the respect of others working in the field, in universities and elsewhere. ... Indeed, if any were to fail entirely in this respect, it would ultimately forfeit its claim to be regarded as a national museum.
>
> This scholarly activity is a major part of the work of senior curators and conservators in a national museum. They are expected to be experts in their field, internationally regarded as authorities. To do their job properly and maintain their international reputation, they need time for research; they must keep abreast of their subject, visit other collections, read widely, contribute to publications, attend conferences and seminars, and play a leading part in their academic community. This research and

this sort of scholarly activity are not luxuries, to be cut when money is scarce. They are fundamental to the role of a great museum (1988: 5–6).

Both the fundamental importance of the academic effort and the recent and largely economic threats to its continuance justify grave concerns among museum professionals and help to explain their sometimes apparently stuffy and élitist over-reaction to attempts to improve museums for the public, which inevitably affect the ability of scholars to pursue their studies quietly.

In addition to this there is the fundamental problem of the inherent impossibility of properly doing what museums supposedly exist to do. Museums around the world are charged to preserve material evidence in perpetuity. This in itself is impossible as we fight all the natural laws which tend inevitably to reduce dust to dust and ashes to ashes. But piled on this impossibility is another which compounds the first. Museums must also give to the visiting public an appreciation of that material evidence, which means showing objects, and sometimes moving objects, and once in a while allowing objects to be handled, all of which contributes to speed the very destruction which museums are there to prevent. Perhaps one of our problems as a profession has been that emotionally and intellectually we have not accepted the impossibility of what we are asked to do. Accepting the inevitable and its effect upon us and our business is usually the first step towards learning to live in peace with it.

The situation we as museum professionals find ourselves in was graphically illuminated for me recently by Andrew Harmon, an American stage director and management training consultant who worked with us in the Royal Armouries on a series of training courses designed to improve creativity and reduce fear of change. He worked out for us the following outsider's analogy of the problem we all face in our work. It is reproduced here with his permission, and I hope will help and amuse you as it helped and amused us.

> Last week I heard the conductor of the London Symphony Orchestra, Michael Tilson-Thomas, in a radio interview. He spoke of the feeling of exhilaration in the concert hall when the ideas of the composer and the ideas of the orchestra unite in performance. This is a perfect example of the result produced when a team of individuals work together, focused by one common purpose: in this case the creating of beautiful music. Delighting, inspiring, transporting an audience.
>
> Imagine what would happen however if, 200 years in the future, audiences no longer came to hear the music or even the players, but to

hear the instruments. And not just any instruments but rare instruments – old, irreplaceable instruments. The older and more fragile the better. The best music still has to be played, and by world class players, but it has to be played from manuscripts written in the composer's own hand on antiques which might, at any moment, disintegrate into piles of matchsticks or ancient scrap metal. Broken strings have to be painstakingly reconstructed from original materials, split reeds replaced from 400 year old bamboo. Suddenly it is not so easy for the orchestra to make such beautiful music together.

Each performance is a nightmare of contradiction. Every time the violin section launches into a cadenza at high speed a vital piece of the nation's cultural heritage is endangered. When one group of critics complain in the press about the havoc the musicians are wreaking on the instruments – 'these irreplaceable national treasures' – the impresario insists, over the conductor's head, that *forte* passages all be played *pianissimo* to avoid further damage. A month later these same critics lament the loss of vitality in 'our once great orchestra' and insist that everything is beginning to sound the same. Soon attendances begin to fall. Sponsorship is mooted and the Arts Council grant is cut.

Meanwhile, inside the organisation, there are 'people problems' everywhere. The instruments are lovingly looked after by the conservation department who are proud of their work and cannot help resenting it every time even one of the wondrous objects must be taken out of their vaults to be played. The musicians also love the instruments but resent what they consider to be arbitrary and unnecessary protection procedures, which interfere with their playing and prevent them from using the instruments expressively. Rehearsals have to be abandoned because of the strain it places on the instruments, the musicians are issued surgical masks and gloves for performances, and glass panels are installed in the concert hall to prevent the audience from breathing on the instruments. Throughout the organisation there breaks out a series of bushfire wars between departments. On one side are those whose job it is to look after the instruments. On the other, those who look after the music. Those in the middle, who have to deal with both sides get caught in the crossfire. Finally, in desperation a management consultant is called in. He analyses the problem and presents his report. It is brief, concise and to the point: 'You are no longer in the Orchestra Business. You are in the Museum Business. 200 years ago the Royal Armouries solved this problem. Give them a call and find out how they did it'.

I hasten to assure you that this last comment was not factually correct, but intended as a spur to our endeavours. What he was trying to teach us is that considerable conflict and disagreement is inevitable in our profession. It cannot and should not be avoided, rather it should be used as a positive force for progress. The important thing is for us to understand that in a complex situation there may be more than one right and legitimate point of view.

However, given all the problems of our profession, given the impossibility of our ultimate duties and given the increasing pressures of our present situation, it is easy to see why the increasing demands of the visitor, or at least the increasing advertisement of those demands, confuse some and worry many others. The spectre of museums as theme parks, of 'Disneyfied' and academically emasculated fun places haunts many, and here too there has been a dangerous polarization of views in recent years, which perhaps hides some fundamental truths. In a recent article in the *Daily Telegraph* (5 October 1990), Richard Dorment suggested that the way to 'save' our museums was to 'sack your market researchers, sack your advertising men . . . and spend the money saved on what museums do well'. This suggests that some special blame attaches to this species for the present state of our museums, which are, so the story goes, in deep crisis. This in my view is a gross distortion of the truth of our situation in many ways, and is both a product of and an incitation to the polarization of views I mentioned above. Such journalistic exaggeration needs to be considered very carefully if we are not to be wrongly affected by it. Do we really believe museums are in crisis? Are they not more active and vibrant with ideas and enthusiasms than ever before? Are the marketing and advertising men really responsible for the ills of museums? Are they not merely the eyes and ears and sometimes the voice of the organization, providing information to help managers manage, and announcing and publishing the results? As a military historian, I hope you will forgive me a military analogy to make the point. The eyes and ears of any army are its scouts. If scouts scout and report accurately but the army command makes a bad decision on the basis of this information and the army is soundly defeated, should one really blame the scouts and call for them to be sacked, and for the employment of more infantry men who do the real fighting?

It is important to realize, as Andrew Harmon was trying to tell us, that there are many people with legitimate roles and points of view involved in museum work. Museum directors have to weigh up the conflicting advice they receive and effect some sort of synthesis. An overemphasis on confrontation and polarization between opposed views and camps does not always help this process, although it is understandable and to a certain extent necessary. However, we need to learn to pull ourselves together rather than apart a little more. As Neil MacGregor has suggested (*The Guardian*, 10 October 1990) the apparent choice between academic excellence and popular accessibility hides a much more fundamental and important truth about museums: 'Scholarship and public access are not alternatives between which museums and galleries must choose: rather it is scholarship that adds a new dimension to accessibility'.

However, there are still many in the profession who do not fundamentally accept that they are employed to serve the 'general' public, and who create for themselves a particular public, an appreciative, sympathetic, important 'academic' or 'specialist' public of their own, to whom their efforts are directed. As Philip Wright has put it:

> On present evidence I fear that many curators do not view the overriding goal of their institution as being to communicate and share knowledge with its visitors, and thus to bring about a diffusion of power and knowledge from the specialist to the non-specialist (Wright, 1989: 134).

This can be a convenient cover for those who see in museums an easy and paid route to pursuing their own hobby and interest, often to the highest level of academic excellence. This attitude still persists, perhaps it always will and should as part of the pantheon of legitimate museum philosophies. Alike for those who agree and disagree with it, is the importance of understanding it, of accepting its existence, and of educating ourselves and others accordingly. The curious set of values and assumptions which this particular attitude both breeds on and leads to is beautifully illustrated in a story told by a trustee of one of our great national collections about a particular keeper in this museum, a man acknowledged for his great and unique contributions to scholarship. Let us call him, for the purpose of anonymity, the Keeper of Sombreros at the National Hat Museum. The following conversation takes place in a long corridor, down one side of which runs a series of large, old, showcases, packed with hats. The Keeper is espied by the Trustee at an open case 're-arranging' it to allow for the inclusion of a new sombrero, by squeezing up those previously on display, and overlapping their brims.

Trustee:	That must be the worst display of hats that I have ever seen.
Keeper:	Yes, it is isn't it?
Trustee:	And you're making it worse by putting something else in.
Keeper:	Yes, but it's so important, extra wide brim and Mitla straw. It's the only one I know of.

Trustee: But you aren't even putting a label in to explain that.
Keeper: (shutting the case). No, but I'll tell you something. With a display like that, anyone who knocks on our department's door to ask about our new sombrero will be someone really worth speaking to.

There is much in this caricature that we can all recognize. Many of the tensions between museum staff and the visiting public are here exposed. Some in the profession would applaud the Keeper's single-minded honesty; most would ridicule him as a caricature of what the profession should not be. Neither reaction is particularly useful. The Keeper in our story is a recognizable archetype, whose existence in museums we must avow, and with whom we must learn to work in order to improve our profession. Fortunately, perhaps, there are many more in the profession who would disagree with him than would agree. Not all museum people fear and disregard the visiting public, and in recent years museums have generally become far more accessible and visitor-orientated places. It is to this that we now turn.

Museums for the public

The improvements in professional training which have been brought about over the last thirty years by the development of graduate and post-graduate university courses, notably at Leicester University, and by the continuing efforts of the Museums Association, have ensured that a growing number of new entrants to the profession are embued with a proper sense of the centrality and importance of public service to the philosophy and purpose of museums. This training has helped new generations of the old museum pro-fessionals – curators and conservators – especially in the non-national museums, to come to terms quickly and constructively with the newer museum professionals – teachers, designers, arts administrators, and so forth – who are as essential as anyone else to the running of museums today. Sometimes this has meant, for instance, the curator of a small museum learning and performing these new skills. National museums have had some widely publicized problems with restructur-ing the organization and responsibilities of the museum between the old and new professionals. One cause of these problems, which has escaped wide publicity, is that the old professionals in national museums still tend to be academic experts of great eminence in their area of study, who are largely untrained in the other ways of the museum profession except by their years of experience. The extension of formalized museum training to all museum staff, old and new, high and low, is now beginning, and is long overdue. It is difficult to see many more major improvements in professional attitudes occurring without it.

Nevertheless, much progress has been made especially in the areas of education, design, public services, and that *bête noire* of many museum people – marketing. I shall deal briefly with each.

Education

The growth in the number of museum staff directly involved in, and trained for, educating the visiting public has been dramatic in recent years. In the twenty-five years from 1963 to 1988, the number of education services in British museums increased almost threefold. Trained teachers working in museums are dedicated to using the collections and other facilities of the museum directly for the public benefit. Their remit goes beyond the requirements of the visiting public, and they are increasingly reaching out into the education system and the community to expand the boundaries of museum work. In their work such staff rarely find themselves in legitimate conflict with the needs of the visitor as sometimes, as we have seen, do curators and conservators, although there may be occasions when the press of visitors hinders education staff from teaching in museum galleries as they would wish. Nevertheless, most museums which have developed educational departments and services in recent years have felt the benefits of adding to their staff numbers of highly committed and motivated communicators. In looking to plan for the needs of visitors now and in future, it is my conclusion and belief that our teachers will play an increasingly important part.

Design

Today many museums still expect their curators to be designers too, and make no provision for trained designers to be involved in the complex and difficult task of displaying and interpreting collections to the public in the galleries, precincts, or parks of the museum. The result of this is the amateur efforts of overworked curators which we still see in too many museums. These amateur efforts range from the commendable to the terrible, and must make all of us once in a while feel embarrassed to be a member of our own profession. Things have been changing, however, although not as fast as some might fondly imagine. My museum, the Royal Armouries, employed its first contract designer only in 1985, and its first in-house designer (responsible for graphic and book design as well as for displays) in 1987. Nor are we alone among the national museums in being tardy. The development of design departments was a phenomenon largely of the late 1970s. The same seems true in local museums – a gradual recognition that display is a separate discipline from curation which requires separate staff to work with the traditional museum professionals to create better and more interesting and informative displays. In the learning process which the development of the necessary team work has involved in all museums, there have, of course, been a number of disasters which has given museum display designers a bad name in some quarters. However, even those who are most outspoken in their criticism of the standard of design in museums today would surely admit that, on balance, it is a vast improvement on the standards of the past, and that the direct beneficiary of these improvements is the museum visitor.

Public services

In recent years many of the larger museums in this country and some of the smaller ones have one way or another created a department or given a member of staff responsibility for the public services of the museum. Areas of responsibility have varied considerably, sometimes even including direct concern for customer care and the training programmes which go with an acceptance that we all need coaching to communicate properly with each other. I suspect that most people so employed see their job more as preserving and organizing the services which the museum has decided to offer the visitor, rather than dealing directly with the visitors themselves and with what they want. However, the development of specialist staff working in this area has been a major advance and has helped to bring a real concern for the public into the main planning and decision making processes of our museums.

Marketing

Here I tread on dangerous ground, for even the word 'marketing' seems enough to send a good proportion of our profession into paroxysms of rage and concern. I nailed my colours to the marketing mast some years ago by writing in the *Museums Journal*: 'The museum profession is a service profession, and we cannot provide a service unless people know we exist, and know the extent of the services we offer' (Wilson, 1988: 98).

Nevertheless, the development of marketing departments in some of our museums and the increasing concerns with marketing among most, are seen by not a few as a sure sign of a possible terminal decline in museum standards. It is true that marketing can be a bottomless pit into which a museum's resources can be dropped with no result. It is equally true, however, that marketing is absolutely essential to all public services, for at root marketing is about the communication between the museum and its public of the legitimate desires and aspirations of both. This is what marketing does for a commercial company too, allowing the company to tell its market what it has to offer, and to find out what the market wants. In this, of course, lies some of the concern expressed by some in our profession. For as well as taking away scarce resources from other areas of museum work, marketing, if carried through properly, involves both the museum and its public in a discussion which should result in an ever-changing synthesis. It involves the museum in change as it responds to the changing requirements of its public. Even if this is simply shown as a great improvement in the quality of services offered, some in the profession seem concerned about the loss of control which is involved in any open negotiation about what we should all be doing. However, in stimulating this debate and making us think, the new emphasis on marketing in museums has done a great service, and has made all of us more aware of the publics which we serve. In making us more conscious of the desires and aspirations of our visitors, the new emphasis surely helps us better to do our job of interesting them in our collections.

The museum visitor

Who are these publics which we serve? If we are to plan for the visitors to our museum we need to know both who they are and why they come. We also need to know many ancillary details such as how many times they come and how long they stay, which is important information for those who have to look after and manage them; and how they come, which is often of importance to those who have to plan cost-effective advertising and public relations campaigns.

Who visits museums?

It is not the purpose of this paper to answer this question, but simply to draw attention to the variety of ways in which it can be answered at a variety of levels and to the importance of doing so. To deal adequately with its visitors every museum should know who they are, for different types of people require different treatment. This is obvious to most of us in the case of the disabled, and most of us realize that men and women require different things from their toilet facilities. But what of children? They have special needs in the galleries and eating facilities of the museum. What of visitors from out of town? They may require car parking facilities which visitors from the locality do not. These are only a few examples to emphasize the importance to us all of knowing precisely what mix of people is visiting our museum so that we can properly prepare for them. Much research has been done in this area in recent years, which varies from that dealing specifically with a single museum, to nationwide surveys of museum visiting trends. These researches are of varying quality and of varying accessibility. Some have been published, some remain the confidential papers of the museum or other organization which undertook them, and others are available on a limited basis.

Occasionally, now, with the increasing interest in this area of museum research, resumés of some of the surveys are published. For instance, five volumes of research data were condensed into three pages for an article which Robert Worcester of MORI and I wrote for the *Museums Journal* in 1988 (Wilson and Worcester, 1988: 37–9). For anyone who wants to know who visits museums, it is important to find and read as many of these reports as possible. They should form the starting-point of many of our decisions for the future. For-tunately, a number of essays have been produced recently discussing museum visitors and what we know of them, and how we find out. In this regard, the work of Eilean Hooper-Greenhill and Nick Merriman has been particularly useful (Hooper-Greenhill, 1988, Merriman, 1989).

What is obvious from all this work is that just under half of the British population visit some sort of museum every year, and that these people tend to be younger, and better educated than the rest of the British public who do not visit museums. Here immediately is an interesting fact for us to consider, for the robust accuracy of these figures has been demonstrated by so many different surveys that it can be called a fact. The result of surveys simply looking at the social class and demographics of museum visitors might well be sufficient on its own to dispel fears that opinion researchers and marketing people were trying to push museums into a demeaning 'Disneyfication'. To do so would appear to run in the face of the evidence that museum visiting is at present – and whether or not we like it – something of an elitist activity. Those who want to find out more about who visits museums, and to follow up many of the interesting lines of thought which this knowledge suggests, must do so in the ways suggested above.

For I now want to say something about the type and quality of work that has and is being done to establish who visits museums. In recent years, professional market researchers have done much good work especially in establishing trends and patterns of museum visitors in general, and more occasionally in linking this with the visitor performance of a particular museum. Their work is now available to guide and help us all. Whether you employ the most expensive research company in the land, or set about doing it yourself, the message I wish to give is plain and clear: it is common sense to know who your visitors are, and professionally negligent not to know. How much information any one of us needs is dependent upon our situation and the particular use to which we wish to put that information. It is important too that we realize that we all have some knowledge of who our visitors are. In the smallest of museums visited by the fewest people in the smallest community the curator and attendant between them may well know the vast majority of the visitors personally, and thus within themselves have the facts they require to make an analysis of their audience. Many museums have visitors' books, in which names, addresses and comments can be written. Few museums demand that visitors sign and so these represent, at best, evidence of a self-selecting portion of visitors to the museum, and statistical evidence gathered from them would need to be so qualified. However, such books do nevertheless represent a source of useful information. Even national museums have altered some of what they do as a result of complaints and suggestions written in a book or dropped into a box. Further, many museums do demand that specific types of visitors sign a book or books. In the Royal Armouries, for instance, we have records of all visits by contractors, volunteers, enquirers and researchers and of those visiting our study collections.

All such records contain very useful information which can be analysed for the benefit of the museum. But how many of us do so? There is much that we can do to help ourselves before turning to sometimes expensive market research companies to do our work for us. What we can do varies from analyzing existing records, through organizing and running simple visitor research in-house, to involving students and staff from a local school, college or university with training in statistical analysis in a joint project of mutual benefit. In any or all of these ways we can find out much more about who is visiting our museums. Why they are coming is a more complex question.

Why people visit museums

Even more important than knowing who is visiting our museums is the question of why they are visiting. The museum visitor is often, even today, defined simply as the paying or non-paying customer who comes to look round the displays, whether permanent or temporary, of the museum. The museum visitor, however, is a more complex phenomenon than this. From the museum viewpoint people visit the institution for a wide variety of reasons to use a wide variety of services, some in the course of their employment, some as a leisure activity. All these should be seen as different kinds of visitors with different requirements. An analysis of museum visitors in this way might give the following provisional list of types (although everyone will I am sure make up a slightly different list).

Contractors/ volunteers	Those people apart from paid staff who visit and work in museums.
Enquirers	Those who make either a planned or casual visit to ask a particular question.
Object owners	Those with an object about which they want an opinion.
Researchers	Those who, whether as part of their employment or as a leisure interest, are engaged in a project which brings them to the museum often more than once. This group could be subdivided into at least three categories depending on which part of the museum's collection they wished to see, viz.: – objects – photographs – archives.

Of course, many will want to research more than one category of the collection, and some may also want to hold discussions with conservation and scientific staff who do not hold direct responsibility for access to the collections.

Students   Those who visit the museum as part of their full or part-time studies. There are many ways in which this group can be subdivided but the ones we tend to use at the Royal Armouries relate firstly to type of student, and secondly to the type of visit, i.e.:

(1) Type of student
 – primary
 – secondary
 – tertiary
 – adult;

(2) Type of visit
 – unaided gallery, i.e. a simple look at the public gallery
 –aided gallery, i.e. using a worksheet or accompanied by a teacher
 – gallery and education centre, i.e. a combination of a gallery tour and teaching in our education centre
 – education centre, i.e. teaching session in the centre only.

Teachers   Those involved in educating others, whether accompanying their students on a pre-visit research trip, or looking for help for a classroom teaching programme.

Gallery users   Those who come to see the objects on display in the museum's public display galleries. These can be usefully subdivided into at least three groups:
 – visitors to permanent galleries
 – visitors to temporary exhibitions
 – visitors who combine visits to both.

Leisure learners   Those who visit the museum and attend its functions in their leisure time, but for primarily educational reasons.

Shoppers	Those visitors who come, chiefly to museums with no entrance charge, simply to shop.
Eaters/drinkers	Those visitors who come, chiefly to museums with no entrance charge, simply to eat and drink.
Event-goers	Those visitors who come to daytime or evening social functions at the museum.

However, in thinking of museum visitors only from the use which they make of the museum's facilities we are considering only half of the issue. For, as we all know, there is often a great deal of difference between what we ostensibly do, and why we really do it. Or to put it another way, the use someone makes of a museum visit may not be the sole or major factor which led to that visit at that time. For instance, free museums are well known in literature and folklore (but less so in reality) as refuges from inclement weather. So the main reason for visiting a museum at a particular time may be to shelter from the rain, but once there one might determine to use the museum for any of the variety of purposes discussed above. For instance, one might determine to enquire about that little mystery which had been puzzling one for some time, or see an exhibition which one would otherwise not quite have summoned up enough interest to go and see.

It might be argued that this is of no concern to a museum professional who is not interested in the subjective compelling reason for visiting, but in the interest and use that results from it. It might, but it surely should not if we do really seek to encourage visitors to visit and learn from the riches of which we are guardians, for an analysis of such reasons can tell us much about how to care for visitors and encourage them to come again. This approach to visitors looks less at *who* they are, or what apparent use they make of the museum, but at the real *reason* for their visiting. It looks at the *psychology* of museum visiting. It is an approach pioneered in North America, and one analysed in some detail by Nick Merriman and Eilean Hooper-Greenhill (see Hooper-Greenhill, 1988: 220–3; Merriman, 1989: 159–70). In the early 1980s Marilyn Hood (Hood, 1981, 1983) identified six major factors contributing to the decisions which adults make about how they use their leisure:

(1) being with people;
(2) doing something worthwhile;
(3) feeling comfortable and at ease in one's surroundings;
(4) having a challenge of new experiences;

(5)   having an opportunity to learn;
(6)   participating actively.

It is against these criteria that visitors will judge what we do in museums, and it is important for us to keep these factors always in our mind. Nick Merriman also argues that there is another and particular reason why people visit museums:

> Museums are associated with 'being cultured' and for various reasons (increased education, increased affluence, desire for improvement of self and children), increasing numbers of people are wishing to participate in such a cultural lifestyle in order to achieve or demonstrate upward social mobility (Merriman, 1989: 168–70).

One does not have to agree with all of the results of this psychological research, to understand that it is an important starting-point both for more research and for action. On balance, it does not seem to me that the recent work of market researchers and psychologists on why people visit museums should lead to anything like the reduction of standards, and trivialization of museums which ill-informed journalists have recently been predicting with increasing vigour and acerbity. Nor, as it happens if they examine wider trends in the leisure industry, is this the way that most other thoughtful businessmen are going either, for they too have access to similar information, and are using it.

What the museum visitor needs

In the last section I identified eleven major different types of museum user. All of these will be concerned with the service or product which they have come to the museum to enjoy. This will apply just as much to those working in the museum as to those who are visiting for pleasure or enlightenment alone. Contractors will be concerned, for instance, to ensure that they are allowed reasonable freedom to go about their job, and will want to be assured that they are properly informed of any essential restrictions before they arrive. Volunteers will be concerned with the quality of work which they are being given, and by the attitude of the permanent staff to them. Researchers, whether paid or unpaid for their research, will want to know in advance what the museum can provide them with, and then will want it provided efficiently and speedily. Enquirers and object owners will want to know when their enquiries will be dealt with, and are likely to be very concerned to ensure themselves that the opinions or facts which they have been given are accurate and reliable. Students (and especially their parents) and teachers will be interested in what is offered by the museum, how it can fit with what they must learn or teach, and how good, reliable, interesting or inspirational the product offered is or will be. Gallery users will be concerned to know what is on show in the museum, when it is not on show, and how it is displayed. Leisure learners, especially, will wish to be inspired by the museum's programme of exhibitions, lecture and special events. Shoppers will be interested in what is for sale, eaters on what there is to eat and drink, and both with the care with which staff treat the users of shops and restaurants. Event-goers will want to be assured of a good quality event and a well organized and pleasant reception of guests. Every type of visitor will want to know far more than this, of course, but these are examples of the areas of concern for each type of museum visitors.

As soon as people know what they want, they have opinions about the level of service they are offered both in general and in particular institutions. To know how well or badly we are doing, we have to ask these users of the services we provide, and this is the fundamental and continuing importance of opinion research. In addition, for that majority of our visitors who come during their leisure time rather than as part of their work we should surely frame the questions we ask to help us discover why people visit either museums in general or ours in particular during their own time, and to test the now seven criteria that have been identified as of special importance:

(1)   being with people;
(2)   doing something worthwhile;
(3)   feeling comfortable and at ease in one's surroundings;
(4)   having a challenge of new experiences;
(5)   having an opportunity to learn;
(6)   participating activities;
(7)   participating in a cultural lifestyle.

Once we have tested these criteria, we may, of course, find them to be inaccurate or inappropriate, but the important point is that there will always be psychological and personal reasons why individuals come to museums which must be considered along with their opinions of the particular services which museums are offering at any one time.

From this point of view, I think that most of us would agree that we actually know very little about the opinions and attitudes of visitors to our museums, in the sense that we have done little formal research into many of the areas I have identified. While that is true of formal opinion research, most of us will have in our heads the results of our own informal opinion researches of the attitudes of visitors, and of course we have something just as valuable and important as the attitudes of others, our own opinions and ideas. This is an important and often forgotten starting point. Very few pieces of market and opinion research undertaken about museums have included research into the attitudes and opinions of staff, and this is a great pity. If you want to find out what the public thinks of a new display, asking the museum's attendants and warding staff can be just as valuable as asking the visitors themselves, for the warding staff witness every day the effect of the display upon the visitors. Similarly, the museum's librarian should be the first person to ask about the level of acceptability of the service currently offered to the public as it will be the librarian who has been in direct contact with the users of that service. I am not, of course, suggesting that this use of staff knowledge alone is sufficient – it will always be at best partial and selective – but I am saying that it is an often neglected and important staging-point to greater and more accurate knowledge of the attitudes and requirements of visitors.

Once the knowledge of staff has been elicited and considered, the need for more formal and accurate information should become more apparent, and the sort of areas of questioning required should become clear. At this stage there is still much which can be done in many areas in-house at little expense. It is quite easy, for example, to construct a simple questionnaire on the organization of an enquiry service, and ask each enquirer to complete it in exchange for the information the enquirer is seeking. When writing a questionnaire for the first time it is sensible if possible to ask for advice from someone who has done it before, and by and large the more experienced they are the better will be their advice. The main thing to remember is that asking a question in the right way is as important as asking the right question. Below, I list a few of the 'do's' and 'dont's' we have learned in the Royal Armouries since we began seriously to consider researching into the opinion of our visitors:

- those being questioned generally do not like to give offence. They will tend to err on the generous side if given the chance. Questions should be framed to give as little opportunity for generosity as possible;

– original ideas rarely come directly from opinion research. If given options those questioned will choose intelligently between them, but will not make up solutions. Thus, avoid questions like 'How would you improve the museum shop?'; instead try a list prefixed by 'Number in order of importance/choose the most important of/the following ideas for improving the museum shop';

– avoid 'cover-all' options as these can badly distort responses. For instance, if you ask those questioned to choose what of a number of reasons for visiting the museum was the most important, and have a cover-all phrase such as 'general historical/artistic interest', you will probably find that this is by far the most popular. On reflection you may well then feel that you are not much further forward;

– beware of questions like 'If we did so and so would you be interested?' The public's generosity tends to provide the answer yes, and can lead to disappointment when you do it and the response is not as great as you had been led to expect. Questions like this need to give specific benefits and or mention a range of charges against which real interest can be measured;

– in attempting to find out what people are prepared to pay for anything, avoid the straight question 'Would you pay x for y?' In addition to the possibility that you may miss the fact that they might be prepared to pay twice as much, real interest in paying can only be measured by comparison with a willingness to pay for something else with the same money, or by offering a range of choices.

These few practical points will, I hope, be of use both to those who want to undertake some research on their own, and to those who are looking to commission market and opinion researchers. In addition, they may help in the equally important analysis of the results of research undertaken. It must be remembered that although the majority of market researchers are very well trained in their own disciplines, most of them will have done little or no work in a museum context, and therefore are more prone to asking the wrong question or to asking the right question in the wrong way when dealing with our problems than when engaged in areas of research more familiar to them. For it is the lack, rather than the quantity, of detailed research on the various aspects of visitor use of museums which is surprising when one begins to look for it, although, as I have suggested, there is more knowledge beneath the surface than is immediately apparent.

Even in such a fundamentally visitor-oriented part of museum work as the public display of collections, very little has been done in this country to analyse the public acceptability of past, current, and future display techniques on anything but a very broad level, and even when such research has been done it is rarely taken note of. My introduction to this phenomenon was twenty years ago when visiting a major museum in the north west which had just opened a gallery specially designed as a didactic teaching display which had to be seen and read in a particular order. The wives of those responsible were used as a control and asked to use the gallery as it had been intended to be used, reading and looking at everything in turn. It took on average twenty minutes to go from beginning to end. Then the attendant staff were asked to monitor the length of time which the public spent in that gallery. The average length of stay was one minute. Something was obviously very wrong. The gallery had failed. Nevertheless, ten years later I noticed that it was still there. It may be there even now. It is perhaps one of the prices the profession has paid for the dominance of curators in the field of public displays which only very recently has come to be questioned.

Thankfully, interest in the subject of how the public reacts to displays is now increasing due both to the development of museum marketing in general and to the pioneering work of one museum, the Natural History Museum, and to one member of its staff, Roger Miles, in particular (Miles, 1989). Roger Miles and his team pioneered a system of market-testing new display ideas before introducing them, and then of assessing them once in place in the major galleries. This is an example of the proper use of research data as part of a process leading to an improved end result and is the antithesis of the visitor research which ends gathering dust on a bookshelf, and which was apparently carried out for cosmetic or political reasons rather than for practical ones. The results are also palpably different from the kind of disaster I mentioned above, which is all too common in most of our museums. That display was almost certainly designed as follows: 'During the entire exhibition process the museum staff... and the visitors remain invisible to each other. There is no contact or communication'. The inevitable result from the visitors' point of view was that 'the displays present a closed system... and there is no possibility of influencing or changing the existing cases or panels' (Hooper-Greenhill, 1988: 229).

The paucity of good research data is even more obvious in other areas of museum work than in that of display where there is a considerable amount worldwide. In the field of museum education, for example, little has been done to ascertain what the teachers, parents and pupils really want from museums that museums can properly and sensibly provide. This may be because we have relied upon the professional knowledge of the teachers employed in museums and have not felt the need to amplify this with consumer research. In 1990 the Royal Armouries sponsored research into the attitudes of teachers and parents to the educational provision at museums and heritage sites in general and at the Royal Armouries in particular. We did this to help us plan our education service over the next five years in the light of changes in education wrought by the introduction of the national curriculum, and by the changing financial situation both of museums, schools and parents. It is intended to publish the results shortly, and here is not the place to discuss the findings. I mention it only as an example of the sort of detailed research into the requirements of particular types of museum visitors which can produce very interesting and useful results. But the interesting only becomes useful and thus justifies the time and money spent on it if it is used. The importance and success of this research into our educational provision, as with all other research, will be judged by the use we make of it, and how we integrate the knowledge we have gained into our plans for the future. It is to this fundamental question that I now turn.

Planning and organizing for action

It is not possible to plan anything unless you know both what you are supposed to be doing in the long term and what people require of you in the here and now. Despite the amount written in recent years on the purpose of museums, I sometimes find both in myself and in others a great deal of confusion about what we are here to do. In part this is an inevitable result of the irreconcilable tensions which rightly exist in our profession and which I mentioned earlier. In part, also, I suspect, it is due to the inevitable fact that those who form the legislative and legal framework within which we work are not museum professionals and that therefore our legal duties are not always entirely consistent with our professional aims and aspirations.

Whatever the reason, I do believe that to allow any of us to plan properly we all need to clarify and articulate our own position and view, and understand, and have understood by others, how they fit into the wider museum picture which must accept a broad range of diverse views as a precondition for properly planning and working together. This is especially important with planning for the visitor, for as I have tried to suggest, we cannot plan properly and reasonably unless we understand that for some in museums the visitor is the reason for their employment, and for others, just as understandably and properly, visitors are an irrelevance.

Apart from an acceptance of what museums are here to do, before we plan properly for visitors we need to understand what our visitors require. This means finding out about them, and their needs, and analysing the information which we have gathered. Opinion research is only a means of gathering information. How it is analyzed and used is the business of the management of the museum. Opinion and market research should always be used as an aid to management not as a form of management. In other words, it is a misuse of opinion research always to do what the results of the research suggest that the public wants. The public may be asking for something which the museum cannot deliver, or through misinformation or prejudice they may simply be wrong. Research is simply a tool to enable us all to ask more questions, the answers to which help us to plan sensible courses of action. It enables us to establish both what the public wants which we can give them, and how great is the gap of understanding between the museum and the public. We do not need to be led into any direction in which we do not wish to go by opinion research. It tells us simply what people think. It is more valid a reaction to organize an educational and public relations campaign in an attempt to change public perception than it is to go unhappily where the wind seems to blow. All that knowledge of what our visitors think can do for us is to help us make sensible and appropriate decisions. Planning and decision taking is both easier and more likely to be correct if it is informed than if it is ignorant.

Planning itself is very simple, but not at all easy. Many books have been written on it, and much ink spilt over it, but in essence there are four stages:

(1) *Gather information*: bring together all the people, ideas and knowledge that are necessary before a sensible decision can be made;
(2) *Decide*: Choose a course of action (or inaction); ensure that the decision is understood by all who need to know about it;

establish a clear line of responsibility for the consequent necessary actions; and set targets, timetables and indicators;

(3) *Monitor*: As work continues, ensure that progress is checked against the agreed targets, timetables and indicators of performances;

(4) *Assess*: Once the agreed action has been completed, it is essential to continue to monitor its effect and to discuss what has been learned, and what went right and wrong. This is essential if planning for the future is to improve. Without assessment the same mistakes are likely to be made again.

This 'process' can be very formal or very informal, but even if we are only setting ourselves a task, the process is one which most of us use almost unconsciously. It can become much more useful if we do it consciously and conscientiously.

I am also convinced that for planning to work properly something more than communication of the planning process is required – and that is involvement. The more all those who work in a museum can be involved in the planning of what the museum does, the more likely is it in my view that those plans will come to fruition. This is not to say that I am advocating industrial democracy in museums. Involvement and understanding is, I believe, both more important and more attainable than agreement, which as I have suggested above is often likely to be a chimera given the irreconcilables with which museums work. What is possible, and what we are working towards at the Royal Armouries, is a system in which everyone is involved in planning their own work and targets within an understood framework of aims and objectives, and in which everyone can make a suggestion for improving or changing what we do or how we do it in the knowledge that it will be carefully considered as part of the normal planning process. If done within a framework of mutual understanding of the different expertises, responsibilities and philosophies of the different types of museum staff, this sort of real involvement and responsibility for planning the work of the museum is a key which can release individual creativity to the benefit of all. For those responsible for the ultimate direction of a museum, the results of involving staff in this way can be profound. However creative and full of ideas a Director or a Board of Trustees or a Committee may be, the more heads that there are thinking positively about a solution to a problem, the more likely it is that a sensible and creative solution will be found.

Of course, these ideas apply to *all* planning, not just planning for visitors. However, given the polarization of views within the profession about how planning for visitors should be handled, and how important it is, the participation and involvement of as many different museum professionals in planning for the requirements of visitors may be one of the best ways to promote the greater level of understanding which seems to be required to ensure constructive synthesis rather than destructive antithesis.

But however good a planning process is, it will not achieve adequate results unless the structures and relationships within the museum and between the museum and its users are adequate and appropriate. In conclusion, therefore, I should just like to pose the following questions, which I believe we all need to be constantly asking and attempting to answer: Is the relationship between the museum and the visitor the right one? Are our working methods good enough to achieve the results we aim for? Is the managerial structure and staff organisation of the museum appropriate? Are we well enough trained for what we have set ourselves to do?

There are no right or wrong answers to these questions; they will vary from time to time and from institution to institution. Asking them can be uncomfortable for it brings us face to face with some contentious issues. I should like to end, therefore, not by giving my views on what the answers should be, but by discussing some of the issues which these questions have raised in my mind recently.

The first question, about the relationship between museum and visitors, can immediately raise the issue of charging for admission. This is not the place to discuss the principles involved in this, but I should like to share a view which was expressed to me during research for this paper by staff from a number of museums which have recently begun to charge. This is that charging for admission has made the museum and its staff more responsive to the visitor who is more likely to complain if the standard of service falls below expectation. The articulation of this suggestion may well be a response to criticisms of charging. The change in staff attitude may be due in large part to such things as customer care courses introduced after charging was instituted. The likelihood of an increase in complaints from people who have to pay for a service seems to be almost self-evident. Nevertheless, there is in all this the question of whether in a museum context the act of charging does irrevocably alter the relation between museum and visitor, and if so in which way. It is an aspect of the great debate on charging which has largely been ignored in favour of discussion of the ethics involved and the reduction in visitor numbers supposedly caused by the introduction of charges. It is an area of interest to any of us who charge for anything, whether general admission, exhibition entrance, shop products, or food and drink. It can involve us in the questions of how we value what we use and how we use what we value, and in the general psychology of the relationship between price and value. Whether or not we are personally comfortable with charging for the services which we provide, we should be interested in the answers to these kinds of questions, and in the new insights which can be gained from looking at an old debate in a new way.

The second question raises the issue of whether our working methods in museums are such as to allow us to achieve what we have set ourselves to do. In terms of the visitor, this means asking whether we are organizing the delivery of visitor services in the way most likely to promote the kind of services which the visitor wants or is persuaded to want. As an example, let me raise again the question of display design. From the earlier quotation about lack of contact between visitors and designers during the design process, it could be concluded that visitor contact and involvement is essential to success. But do we really believe this? From the number of poor and inadequate displays we have seen which have been the result of the exclusion of visitors from the design process, we might conclude that it was. But is this reasonable and logical? What of the analogy with the stage or film director and his creative team? They rarely, if ever, undertake opinion research beforehand. They sometimes, but not always, have a pre-opening or pre-release test run to allow for minor alterations to be made. But fundamentally they operate strictly on a closed system, with the director ultimately responsible for the delivery to the audience of a product which the audience finds acceptable.

Most of the time this system works, sometimes it does not, depending largely on the skill and competence of the creative and organization talents involved, and partly on the luck of timing, and thus relevance, of the message and its form. Of course, this may not be a fair analogy, but it perhaps should make us pause and think before recruiting member of the visiting public as the *vox populi* on every design team. The important thing to realize, surely, is that if we are designing public displays, these displays must be capable of delivering to the public the message which we intend them to deliver. This may require public participation, and indeed this has been experimented with by a number of American museums who have included a member of the public on display teams. On the other hand, it may require good research such as that provided at the Natural History Museum. Or it may require the participation in the display project team of a trained interpreter, communicator or teacher (at the Royal Armouries we now have a member of our education staff on every display team). Or it may require the employment of someone with training in psychology. Or it may necessitate training staff in some of the psychology of communication and learning. Fundamentally, it requires all of us to understand what is required and to work without prejudice in any particular situation towards the optimum way of providing the best possible service or product to the visiting public.

The third question reminds us of the importance of the management structure of a museum. Any organizational structure must be linked to the aims and objectives of the museum, for the structure is simply the way the institution is organized to achieve its purpose. If the purpose of the organization or its priorities change considerably, then the management structure will almost certainly have to change as well. This is what has been happening in many of our national museums in recent years as they adapt to changing perceptions of their roles and duties. In museums everywhere the changing perceptions of the importance of the visitor have led to changes in staffing with the introduction of the newer professionals with marketing, display and teaching skills. In the large museums these new staff have been formed into new departments, which have affected the overall organizational structure of the museums.

Usually staff have been organized into additional specialist departments increasing the number of skill-based compartments into which museums have traditionally been split. However, functional departments, dealing with such things as visitor services and customer care, have more recently been established in some museums, sometimes consisting of staff taken from a number of skill-based departments. This has led others to begin to consider whether skill-based compartmentalization is the best and most appropriate structure for the future, or whether cross-specialist functional departments should become the norm. In the Royal Armouries we have retained our skill-based structure, but now increasingly work in interdepartmental project teams with staff from different specialisms drawn together as appropriate for the particular task in hand. This hybrid organization is not uncommon today. Others have considered, and are beginning to introduce, more radical approaches. Some multi-site museums now see the ideal organization of the future as being like a central holding company controlling certain common services with a number of operating companies, in the form of separately organized, staff and financed visitor attractions, overtly or covertly competing against each other. This is not the place to argue the merits or demerits in principle of any of these approaches. I prefer to take the pragmatic view that we should all be looking for whatever will work for us in our particular circumstances. What is important to stress here is that the visitor to museums will only be properly considered, planned for, and looked after if the needs of the visitor are properly considered in the planning process of the museum, which, in turn, will not be the case if the organizational structure does not give proper weight and status to those with direct responsibility for the visitor.

The fourth and last question asked whether we are well enough trained. Despite continuing improvements in the provision of the training of museum professionals the answer must be no, and almost certainly always should be no, for training is surely so important that we should never be satisfied that it is sufficient, however good it may be. In the absence of proper training on the needs of visitors, the principles and practice of good communication, the psychology of learning, and the like, we have often to rely on consultant designers, interpreters, communicators, psychologists, and the like, and because of our own lack of knowledge we find it difficult, if not impossible, to manage them, for we cannot judge good from bad advice, nor recognize good from bad performance. This is surely the fundamental importance of training, that it must both allow us to perform our own specialisms better, and give us sufficient grounding of knowledge in the specialisms of others to allow us to work with them and manage them for the benefit of the museum. Properly to plan for, and look after, visitors requires skills and specialisms which, despite the fact that museums have always been in the business of looking after visitors, have not been traditionally seen as essential for a museum career. This attitude is changing. The sooner it changes and all museum professionals are properly trained so that they can identify each other's legitimate but different points of view, the sooner will the museum visitor be properly considered and treated, and the sooner will more museums begin to fulfill their real potential and true role in society.

Acknowledgement

I am indebted to the following for help and comments during the preparation of this paper: Elizabeth Esteve Coll, Neil Cossons, David Blackmore, Peter Hammond and Richard Ormond. The errors and prejudices within the paper, however, remain entirely mine.

Bibliography

Hood, M.G., *Adult Attitudes Towards Leisure Choices in Relation to Museum Participation*, PhD thesis, Ohio State University, 1981.

Hood, M.G., 'Staying away – why people choose not to visit museums', *Museum News* 61 (4) 1983: 50–7.

Hooper-Greenhill, Eilean, 'Counting visitors or visitors who count' in *The Museum Time Machine* R. Lumley (ed.) (London, 1988): 213–32.

Merriman, Nick, 'Museum Visiting as a Cultural Phenomenon' in *The New Museology*, P. Vergo (ed.) (London, 1989): 119–48.

Miles, Roger (ed.), *The Design of Educational Exhibits*, 1989. (Allen and Unwin: London, 1989).

Museums and Galleries Commission, *The National Museums: The National Museums and Galleries of the United Kingdon* (HMSO: London, 1988).

Wilson, Guy and Worcester, Robert, M., 'The role of research in the planning process of the Royal Armouries', *Museums Journal* 88 (1) 1988: 37–9.

Wilson, Guy, 'Marketing and self promotion in museums', *Museums Journal* 88 (2) 1988: 97–f100.

Wright, Philip, 'The quality of visitors' experiences in art museums', in *The New Museology*, P. Vergo (ed.) (London, 1989).

5

Reflections on the social and economic impact of the Fortress of Louisbourg

PATRICIA E. KELL

Introduction

The Fortress of Louisbourg[1] National Historic Park, tucked away in a remote corner of Cape Breton Island in Nova Scotia, Canada, is a wonderful place. It is the archetypical historic site, full of the sights and sounds and smells of an eighteenth-century French fortress. Indeed, a quarter of the old town stands resurrected, peopled once more with the aristocrats, labourers and soldiers who roamed its streets over two hundred years ago. Louisbourg is also an example of a living history site that has tried to do everything right. A tremendous amount of research went into the original reconstruction and that research has been supplemented with ongoing historical investigations in support of the interpretive programmes. The staff are carefully selected and trained; the costumes are exact. It is not surprising that Louisbourg is the flagship of the historic sites system in Canada.

Paradoxically, where many museums and museum-like institutions are founded with altruistic or humanitarian goals – to educate the public or to collect and preserve significant examples of our heritage – Louisbourg was founded with primarily economic benefits in mind. The initial construction was planned to give jobs to men losing their positions in local mines and the whole project was initiated in an effort to diversify the economy of a region which had previously relied almost exclusively on fish and coal. Tourism was proposed as a means to enhance the financial prospects of Cape Breton.

In an age when the aims of the heritage industry are seen to be overshadowing the more philanthropic goals of historic sites, it is worth reviewing the experiences at Louisbourg and evaluating them in terms of their success on the economic and social level. An examination of the site reveals that it has succeeded in ways far beyond the expectations of those who first proposed the project: it has indeed developed into a historic site that is far more than what Neil Cossons has called a 'stage set for tourism' (Cossons, 1985). However, despite the definite professional and economic merits of the project, there remain difficulties on the social plane. Although it was initiated and financed by the central Canadian government, official policy has found itself at odds with the philosophy and priorities of the local people. Thus, like many imperialist ventures, it has succeeded in the objectives it set for itself but has failed to sell its goals to the people on whom they were imposed. This paper will examine the history of the site, both distant and recent, the economic impact of the reconstruction on the local economy and the social impact that has accompanied the financial good.

The phoenix risen from the ashes

In 1713 the War of the Spanish Succession came to a close and peace was formalized with the Treaty of Utrecht. France had been defeated and was obliged to cede its holdings on mainland Nova Scotia and Newfoundland to the British. It retained, however, Prince Edward Island and Cape Breton, and Louisbourg was built to become the capital of this new colony. Set on the shore of a deep harbour, near the great stocks of cod and the entrance to the St Lawrence, the town had many natural advantages both for commerce and defence. Over the next several decades, the settlement flourished into the largest fortress (fortified town) in North America. Meanwhile, the astounding bureaucracy of pre-revolutionary France made copious and detailed notes about the buildings, legal proceedings and business transactions.

The peace between Britain and France was short-lived. In 1745, Louisbourg was besieged and lost but returned to the French in the subsequent peace treaty. Again in 1754, war broke out. Louisbourg was once more attacked and fell in 1758. This time the French colony was retained by the English and, having themselves founded Halifax as an alternate seat of maritime defences, they blew up what remained of Louisbourg in 1763 and deported all its inhabitants.

Louisbourg lay in rubble for almost two hundred years, while an English town, also called Louisbourg, grew up on the far side of the harbour. The site was recognized and protected as a historic site in 1928 and a museum placed there in 1930 (Fortier and Fitzgerald,

1979). However, real interest in the location did not develop until 1960, with the decline of the coal industry. The government of Canada appointed a royal commission to investigate what could be done to help the decaying situation, and rather than try to regenerate the coal mines, the report suggested that the economy be broadened to appeal to the tourist market. It read in part:

> Here are resources of profundity as well as enjoyment; the scenes are a national property to be brought to the attainment of their potentialities. What is proposed will be not only of economic benefit to the Island; it will introduce elements to regenerate its life and outlook, dissolve the climate of drabness and let into human hearts and intelligence the light of new interests, hopes and ambitions (Rand, 1960: 46).

What Rand proposed was to rebuild a portion of the Fortress. This would give the unemployed miners jobs and teach them new skills which might be marketable. In 1961 the Federal Cabinet approved the twenty-five million dollar restoration project (Fortier and Fitzgerald, 1979).

Even at the time of the project's proposal, some argued that the money would be better spent preserving buildings which were still standing rather than recreating a lost town (Fortier, 1981). However, the idea of the project was not necessarily to do the greatest good for the preservation of Canada's heritage; it was to create jobs in a depressed area of the country. Of course, this money-centred view of heritage management was couched in some more altruistic rhetoric. Judge Rand, for instance, maintained that the reconstruction would 'bring fresh and heightened scenes and an evaluation of the mind and spirit to its people' (1960: 46).

The millions of dollars certainly brought change. Where once there was rubble, there now stand fine stone houses, a great bastion, the walls of the city, the moat, the quay, and even a typical boat riding at anchor in the harbour. And perhaps most to Louisbourg's credit through this rebuilding phase was the attention to historical evidence and accuracy. The hundreds of thousands of documents produced by the French government during the period of occupation were meticulously researched and employed during reconstruction. Further, archaeological teams unearthed many more useful pieces of material evidence about the past. The investigations produced a considerable quantity of original research (for example, Larrabee, 1971; Lindsay, 1975), and the publications generated by the site have included several by superintendents on the running of historic sites (Lunn, 1972; Fortier, 1981).

Today, with about a quarter of the town reconstructed and no plans to rebuild more, the public programme is impressive. Costumed animators people the town, portraying the lives of the former inhabitants. Apart from soldiers demonstrating the typical military drills, the fishermen clean fish, children play period games and, in recent years, a band of minstrels occasionally provides entertainment in the inn. During the summer, a series of evocative evening concerts is held in the bastion performed by professional musical groups specializing in period music. Perhaps the most impressive feature of this array of activity is that, before any presentation appears on the site, it must be approved by a committee composed of historians, material culture specialists and visitor activities staff. There is clear commitment to the attempt to present as accurate a picture of the past as possible. This is not to say, of course, that the site is beyond the criticisms applicable to all historic sites: there are some parts of the past that are not shown and the past is never totally recreated. However, by working with what is known and focusing the animation programme on a single year (1744), considerably more can be revealed than would be possible at a site composed of buildings from different locations or portraying a breadth of time.

The Fortress of Louisbourg has reappeared from the foggy depths of time. It is no longer the capital of a French colony but in many ways it has become the capital of historic parks in Canada. Through fortuitous circumstances surrounding its original building and destruction and its subsequent reconstruction, it has come to embody many of the best qualities of a historic site. As an academic institution, Louisbourg is clearly a success: the coal industry's loss is museology's gain. But the very success of the site professionally begs the related questions: has it been so successful in stimulating the economy, and how have the people whom it was intended to benefit reacted to its presence?

Sowing the seed of prosperity

The Louisbourg reconstruction project in its first stages was to be entirely funded by the central Canadian government. Today the Fortress generates some income in its own right, particularly through the introduction of the volunteer association concessions on site and entrance fees to the park. However, the primary source of funding remains direct financing by the federal government. Visitation to Louisbourg is believed to have spin-off benefits for the community as a whole through tourist spending. Interest in the community benefit of tourism is evident in a new initiative to increase visitation to the site as part of a larger regional tourist destination. Like most museums, the site remains financed by the public but the existence of the tourism generated by the site reduces the amount the government would have to spend to support an otherwise depressed area.

Any consideration of Louisbourg as a financial prospect must begin with a consideration of its location. As mentioned earlier, the Fortress was ideally suited for its eighteenth-century purposes: near cod and the major routes of navigation and defence of the Gulf of St Lawrence. However, in the last two hundred years transportation technology and the human geography of North America have changed drastically and what was once on the major highway has become tucked away in a remote corner. Louisbourg is situated about four hours drive from the nearest major city, Halifax. Indeed, there is only one road to Louisbourg and it ends when it gets there. In terms of historic atmosphere, this remoteness has advantages: unlike some other historic sites in Canada, there are no highways looming overhead or skyscrapers invading the historic panorama. In terms of marketing to the tourist industry, however, Louisbourg's location is one of its biggest drawbacks: when you get to Louisbourg you have come to the edge of the New World.

None the less, people do come to visit Louisbourg. The animation programme is only in effect from June to September, with tours of the outdoor parts of the site in May and October. Despite this short season, in 1990 over 115,000 visited the site. Of these, significant numbers came both from bus tours and school groups. To Louisbourg's advantage is the fact that the study of Nova Scotia history plays an important part in the curriculum of grade six students in the province. Thus, although there is no requirement for them to visit, the site is inundated by school groups through most of June. By far the greatest number of people come not in organized groups but on their own – in 1988 about 85 per cent.

An entrance fee is in effect at the site and has been for a long time. It operates on a scale, with concessionary prices for children and families. Senior citizens and children under five are admitted free.

The cost for an adult is less than admission to a film and considerably less than the cost of a visit to Colonial Williamsburg. In 1990, entrance fees totalled almost $400,000. Ironically, because Louisbourg is part of the Canadian Parks Service which is, in turn, part of the Department of the Environment, the site does not keep what it collects in revenue. That money is turned over to the central Treasury. The budget for the site is then decided on by the government and that sum returned to the site. The Fortress therefore does not necessarily benefit directly from increasing the amount of money it takes in at the door.

The second source of income on the site is the concessions system run by the volunteer association. Apart from doing some programming work on and off the site, including organizing costumed children's programmes on the site in the summer months, the volunteers run a series of money-making ventures. These include a gift shop (specializing in Louisbourg-specific memorabilia ranging from playing cards to replica dinner ware), a bakery, and three period restaurants. These operations in 1990 took in about half a million dollars. Unlike the money collected in entrance fees, the funds generated by the volunteer association can be put to work directly at the Fortress.

When the amounts collected in admission fees and through the volunteer association enterprises are compared with the operating budget for the Fortress, it is clear that the operation comes nowhere near paying its own way. Less than one fifth of the funds necessary to keep the site functioning are brought in. In this sense, the reconstruction project has failed to create self-sustaining employment. Rather than creating a profitmaking independent business, the government has obligated itself to an enterprise which will probably never bring in as much money as is required to maintain it. In this sense it is like most other museums. The jobs which have evolved from those first positions created for displaced miners in 1960 still require support from the federal government in order to exist. Having invested the money in the research and reconstruction of the Fortress, the government is unlikely to withdraw its support now, but the economic success of the project is not direct: in terms of balancing the books for the Fortress itself, it is a failure; but in terms of creating some economic benefit to the region, it has succeeded. The extent of this success is not clear as figures reflecting tourism centred primarily on Louisbourg are not available. Clearly, though, Cape Breton is not a prosperous region and any money generated locally through tourism reduces its dependence on the rest of the country through programmes to equalize the nation's wealth.

Louisbourg is probably the best-known historic site in Canada. It is much photographed and the images of it appear on everything from travel posters to picture calendars of Canada. On a recent brochure publicizing Canada's historic sites (of which there are over a hundred) of the approximately eighty pictures, over fifteen were identifiably of Louisbourg ('Discover yourself in Canada's National Historic Sites', 1986). Having made the investment to restore the picturesque town, it is now taken advantage of in order to promote national attention and, ultimately, tourism.

The latest initiative by the Canadian Parks Service is to promote the five heritage sites on Cape Breton as a group tourist destination. The other sites are the St Peter's Canal, Marconi National Historic Site, the Alexander Graham Bell Museum, and Cape Breton Highlands National Park. Of these, the last is by far the largest and the only one that focuses on natural as opposed to cultural heritage. The marketing strategy seeks to sell the island as a tourism destination based on value – a single place offering diverse opportunities to the visitor. The decision to market the island based on benefits to the users is seen as the new direction in heritage institution management:

> Awareness and support of the parks by the public, the numbers of visitors, and the quality of their experience, have been secondary concerns. The organization [Canadian Parks Service] now recognizes the need to balance its traditional role of conservation with an enhanced effort to address visitor needs and satisfaction, and to generate greater awareness for the Program (McArthur, Thompson and Law Advertising, 1989).

The strategy therefore seeks to increase visitation, awareness of the parks' programmes and support for the parks among the local people. In support of this plan two new publications have appeared: a 'Vacation Planner' (1990), full of details about the activities and operating hours of the parks; and a glossy brochure entitled 'Unforgettable' (1990), with a lot of pictures of people enjoying themselves and inspirational prose. For example, in the section on Louisbourg a quotation, apparently attributable to one of the guides reads, 'The instant you walk through the fortress gates and hear the chatter of busy town folk, smell the bracing salt air and see soldiers at drill, you'll have to pinch yourself to be sure you're not dreaming'.

This quotation forces us to confront the difference between living history critics, who insist that what sites present is so far from the reality of past life that it only purports to portray the past, and marketing specialists who believe that what sites offer to people is an experience, the opportunity to see and perhaps feel what it was like to live in the past. Louisbourg has answered both the trend of the last few decades to focus on accuracy in presentation, and the trend of this decade to focus on consumer orientation and marketing, although the extent to which this solves the tension between marketing and the myth of accuracy remains, at best, a very open question.

Linked with this is the question of whether Louisbourg is destined to suffer hard times in the coming years. As the cost of petrol increases and technology improves, it will become less and less attractive to go to Louisbourg. The cost of travel will be an effective deterrent to people from making long vacation trips, or at least from making as many of them. It will be important then for Louisbourg, in a remote corner of the country to be one of the destinations of choice. Coming second or third on the list may mean that it is not visited at all. Further, technology offers many forms of gripping entertainment in competition with the site visit, not to mention the threat posed by commercial 'heritage' entertainments which are not constrained by concerns like being in the appropriate location or being accurate. All these arguments support the adoption of an aggressive marketing strategy for places like Louisbourg where the extra effort needed to get there should be rewarded with the added benefit of knowing that one has had the 'real' experience, through the application of first-rate research and presentation methods.

From its beginning as a make work project, Louisbourg has expanded to become a cornerstone of the tourist economy in Cape Breton. While visitation to the site itself comes nowhere near paying for the cost of the attraction, even with the revenue generated by the volunteer association and entrance fees, profits generated in the community in general, from hotel and restaurant patronage and the visitation of other attractions, contribute to the broader economy of the island. In recognition of this spin-off benefit, the government is now devoting money to increase visitorship to the Fortress and thereby increase benefits to the community. The effort that has previously been expended in producing a quality heritage site facilitates its marketing.

Impact on the community

A major public works project such as the reconstruction of the Fortress cannot be effected without having an impact on the community. In the case of Louisbourg, this impact has left long-lasting feelings of both approbation and hostility in the community. The jobs created by the site have given employment opportunities at favourable terms to many in the community. However, to those who are excluded, feelings of hostility, based on dissatisfaction with both the Fortress' language policy and the importation of labour from outside the immediate community, continue to influence their perception of the project. This dissatisfaction leads to broader questions about who the museum should and does serve and in what capacity.

The Fortress offers jobs to many in the community, with a variety of types of job skills represented. There are currently eighty-two full-time year-round staff, about thirty-five people who work for four- to six-month terms, and about a hundred and twelve people who work for three- to four-month terms. This last group is almost entirely made up of the staff who act as guides and animators during the summer visitor season. While it may seem to those in more economically prosperous areas that a job for only three or six months of the year is not particularly desirable, within the Cape Breton context it is not unusual. One of the other large industries on the island is fishing, which is also seasonal. Further, by working for three months at the Fortress and collecting unemployment insurance for the rest of the year, interpreters can make more than, for example, a bank teller in the neighbouring town of Louisbourg.

The jobs at the Fortress are clearly considered desirable by the local inhabitants. Indeed, this is the source of some of the tension surrounding the Fortress. Three problems will be examined here. First, not all people hired at the Fortress are hired on the same terms, leading to disgruntlement among those who are paid less for similar work. Second, because the Fortress tries to provide services in both official languages, some anglophones in the immediate region of the Fortress feel displaced by francophones brought in from further afield. Finally, because the Fortress is a leading historic site, often skilled professionals are brought in to research and management positions from outside the local community.

The Fortress hires summer staff in at least three ways. The

Canadian Parks Service, or the park itself, hires most of the interpretive staff on site. These people are the best paid interpretive employees. The government also hires students through a summer job programme. While these people are paid relatively well compared to other summer jobs, particularly those available on Cape Breton, even students pursuing doctorates would not receive as much as the formal park employees. Finally, the volunteer association hires people to work in costume on site in the restaurants and bakery. Although these people appear to visitors to be indistinguishable from the parks employees, they are paid considerably less. Clearly then, it is not surprising that some tensions arise between the members of these various groups and that the hostility is often focused on the park for not hiring all equally. It should be noted, however, that this situation – where people are hired on a number of different contracts and paid different amounts – is very common at Canadian Parks Service sites and parks.

A further result of this ongoing tension about interpretive positions is that volunteer activities on the site are restricted. Under no circumstances may an unpaid person take over the position of a salaried employee, since it is perceived that the salaried position will then be lost. While there are occasions when volunteers do appear on site in costume, most notably the annual festivities for the Fête de Saint-Louis they focus most of their work off site.

A second source of tension within the community stems from the Fortress' policy to try to hire 60 per cent bilingual (English and French) staff in interpretive positions. This is an outgrowth of the federal government policy to offer all government services in both of the nation's official languages. Clearly, in a historic site portraying a settlement which was originally French, there is justification both from the point of view of accurate historical presentation and in recognition of the fact that many of those who would be most interested in the site might be francophone.

On Cape Breton Island, while many of the original settlers were of Scottish extraction, there are areas of Acadian French. These people are not descendants of the original inhabitants of the Fortress. Many of the bilingual interpreters at the site come from these villages, which, for the most part, are on the far side of the island from Louisbourg. Difficulties arise because people in the area surrounding the Fortress itself, and particularly in the town of Louisbourg, feel that they are excluded from employment at the site in favour of these people. As was the case with differential hiring arrangements on site, the problem of tensions based on linguistic differences and the federal government's policies towards bilingualism are not peculiar to Louisbourg. Indeed, the insistence of the government on bilingual services has been one of the most contentious issues in Canadian politics over the past fifteen years and is unpopular with large segments of the anglophone Canadian population. For the French, on the other hand, access to services in their native language is seen as a necessary part of being equal members of the nation.

The inherent conflict between regionalism and nationalism as manifest in language was illustrated at Louisbourg last year when the area from which the Fortress tried to recruit interpretive staff was enlarged to incude all of Nova Scotia and New Brunswick. This was done with the express purpose of trying to find more bilingual staff. The results did not offset the increased time and effort involved in the wider search and this coming summer the area will revert once again to Cape Breton Island alone. This example points out emphatically that the language issue can and does have a significant influence on who gets jobs and hence is a source of conflict between the site and its surrounding community.

The final area of tension between the Fortress and its community over hiring practices revolves around the need to hire professional staff from outside the region. While some of the highly-qualified staff have been native Cape Bretoners, many of the historians, curators and managers have been imported from across the country. As these are the best paid and most influential jobs at the site, it is not surprising that there is some sensitivity about who fills them. The tension is exacerbated by the practice of housing many of these people in a subdivision separate, and incidentally geographically above, the main town of Louisbourg. Perhaps these tensions are typical of large businesses in small towns but the Fortress has none the less failed to relax them.

All these problems point to a single question: who was this project designed to benefit? If it was the local community through the creation of the maximum number of jobs possible, then perhaps the employment equity problems are understandable. If it were the nation, then the insistence on pervasive use of French and the hiring problems that connotes are acceptable. And if it were the heritage community, then the need to hire highly trained professional staff cannot be denied. The roots of the reconstruction project as a make work project clearly indicate that the local community has been one of the prevailing concerns. However, the Fortress was designed not to give a job to everyone on the Island but to stimulate the tourist industry in order to create jobs in the private sector as well. In order to be most successful in terms of a tourist attraction, which may include both being professionally recognized as significant and being socially correct on the level of visitor services, the direct interests of the local community are not necessarily served. The problem of balancing these interests is a delicate one.

This model of institutional management contrasts sharply with the 'ecomuseum', or community museum, concept. In the ecomuseum, local residents decide jointly on the significance of local heritage resources and the way in which they will be presented and interpreted. In the case of the Fortress of Louisbourg, the inception of the idea and all subsequent major managerial decisions have been taken by people other than the local residents. If the ecomuseum is the republican 'by the people, for the people' ideal, then Louisbourg must be its imperial 'by the distant central government, purportedly for the people' antithesis. Where in the ecomuseum it is the heritage of the people in the local community that is presented, in Louisbourg there seem to be no such feelings of ownership among the local people. Louisbourg, as a reconstructed French fortress is a national treasure and one which the national government oversees; it is not the expression of the heritage commitment of the community and, as such, it cannot be expected that the local community is entirely in agreement with its policies and actions.

Conclusion

Most heritage institutions are guided by mandates that outline their role as guardians, researchers and disseminators. They exist for the edification and education of academics and of the visiting public. The Fortress of Louisbourg has similar goals, including that it should be 'for the benefit and enjoyment of the people' (Parks Canada, 1979). Such rhetoric should not, however, be confused with the sometimes more pragmatic reasons why institutions come into existence. Such was the case with Louisbourg where local economic problems fostered the establishment of a historic site of national importance. Unusual as this may seem for a heritage institution, it is strangely parallel to the founding of the Canadian Parks Service itself. In 1885, the first park, Banff, was set aside as a national park but much of the impetus to save this area of wilderness was prompted by the Canadian Pacific Railway Company which had recently put a line of track directly through that section of the mountains. It was believed that the creation of the park would encourage people to use the rail line and so the national park system was born.

Much as Banff has grown beyond the interests of the railway company to become an international symbol of nature preserved, so Louisbourg has grown beyond the needs which caused its founding. No longer are the goals of the park largely related to the local people. The scholarly community has expressed its interest in, and approbation of, the site since its completion and significant work continues to be done. Increasingly, the interests of the visiting public are being considered and the site is represented to the general populace as both an exciting tourist destination and as a significant symbol of the history of Canada. All of this leaves the local community to fall victim both to the vicissitudes of national politics and to the necessities of professionalism.

The story of the relationship of Louisbourg to its local economy is one of success: the Fortress has brought, and continues to bring, money to a part of the country which needs it. The economic need which spurred the reconstruction of the Fortress has fostered further success in the field of heritage interpretation, creating a site which is noteworthy and respected on the national level. The only level on which this economic plan has failed is in selling the vision of Louisbourg to the people of the local community not as a single employer but as the creator of an interest and investment which reaches far beyond the walls of the Fortress and into the private economy of the community and the communal national psyche.

Acknowledgement

I should like to express thanks to Anne O'Neill of the Fortress of Louisbourg for providing current statistical data on visitation to the Fortress.

Note

1. My own experiences with Louisbourg stem primarily from a three-month period of research which I undertook there. The following reflections are the result of my discussions with employees and non-employees of the Fortress and my own observations of life in this community.

Bibliography

Cossons, N., 'Postlude' in *Proceedings of the First World Congress on Heritage Presentation and Interpretation*, J. Lunn (ed.), Heritage Interpretation International (Banff, 1985): 343–9.

Fortier, John, 'Louisbourg: managing a moment in time' In, P.E. Rider (ed.), *The History of Atlantic Canada: museum interpretations*, National Museums of Canada (Ottawa, 1981): 91–123.

Fortier, John and Fitzgerald, Owen, *Fortress of Louisbourg* (Oxford University Press: Toronto, 1979).

Larrabee, Edward, *Archaeological Research at the Fortress of Louisbourg, 1961–1965*, National and Historic Parks Branch (Ottawa, 1971).

Lindsay, Charles S., *Lime Preparation at 18th-century Louisbourg*, Parks Canada (Ottawa, 1975).

Lunn, J., 'Louisbourg the emerging touchstone', *Canadian Antiques* 7, 1972: 37–41.

McArthur, Thompson and Law Advertising and Public Affairs, *Canadian Parks Service Integrated Marketing Strategy and Action Plan*, 1989.

Parks Canada, *Parks Canada Policy* Parks Canada (Ottawa, 1979).

Rand, I.C., *Report of the Royal Commission on Coal* (Ottawa, 1960).

PART TWO

6

'Like a game of dominoes': Augustus Pitt Rivers and the typological museum idea

WILLIAM CHAPMAN

Introduction

Perhaps no other figure so fully conjures up a picture of Victorian anthropology – and anthropological museums – as Augustus Pitt Rivers (1827–1900).[1] Pitt Rivers, of course, is best known for his ideas on museum arrangement, as exemplified in two separate collections formed in his lifetime, and for his pioneering archaeological work, much of which took place on his own estate on the border of Dorset and Wiltshire during the 1880s and 1890s. He is also important, though less well recognized, for his work on behalf of anthropological societies and organizations and as one of the principal founders and architects of the Royal Anthropological Institute, the main professional organization for the field, at least in Britain, since 1871. It was, furthermore, through one of Pitt Rivers' collections, donated to Oxford in 1883, that anthropology first attained a secure foothold in the universities; the conditions of his gift required the appointments initially of Henry Moseley (1844–91) and later of Edward Burnett Tyler (1832–1917) as Curator and Reader respectively. It was, therefore, by this means that anthropology first came to be formally 'taught' in a university setting in Britain and eventually gained academic recognition, if not always respectability (Plate 1).

The general outline and tenor of Pitt Rivers' museum ideals are well known today. He was foremost the father of what has come to be known, after his own designation, as the 'typological' system of museum organization.[2] In general, such a system called for a grouping of ethnographical or archaeological materials according to perceived formal or functional similarities, rather than according to their place of origin, or the 'geographical system', as is more conventional among anthropological museums today. In Pitt Rivers'

Plate 1 Retouched photograph, showing Augustus Henry Lane Fox Pitt
Rivers (1827–1900), taken *c*1880. Photograph: courtesy of the
Pitt Rivers Museum, Oxford.

system, examples of 'primitive spears' would be displayed together in order that the viewer might make comparisons among different types, rather than among a more complete selection of the material culture of a single society. Similar comparisons were made within other ideal categories, such as bows and arrows, fishing implements, housing types (as represented by diagrams and models), baskets and so on. Carried to its logical conclusion, such a system was meant to present a comprehensive history of technology, one with what we would now recognize as an implicit Western European bias. Furthermore, as Pitt Rivers explained his system, it was intended to show the 'progress' or 'evolution' of technology and to instil in the viewer a proper appreciation for the uniform character of changes in the material arts and the 'gradual progress' in technology over time. There were, in Pitt Rivers' terms, 'no sudden jumps' in man's development; (Pitt Rivers, 1891: 116) 'progress' was gradual and at times barely perceptible, both within the modern world and among the more 'primitive' peoples, both modern and historic (or prehistoric). It was, as he explained, 'like a game of dominoes, [in which] like fits onto like; . . . all we know, is that the fundamental rule of the game is sequence' (Pitt Rivers, 1874b: 435). His collections were designed to make that point clear.

The political, or as we might in this context label it, ideological overtones of Pitt Rivers' museum ideas were explicit, or came to be so increasingly. Towards the end of his life Pitt Rivers presented his scheme as a check on 'scatterbrained revolutionary suggestions' and a source of stable reference to a fast-changing world (1891: 116). As he explained at a meeting of the Society of Arts in 1891:

> The knowledge of the facts of evolution, and of the processes of gradual development, is the one great knowledge that we have to inculcate, whether in natural history or in the arts and institutions of mankind; and this knowledge can be taught by museums, provided they are arranged in such a manner that those who run may read (1891: 116).

Holding his scheme as outside of conventional politics – 'the student of science can be neither exclusively Liberal nor exclusively Conservative', he explained earier (1884: 15) – he saw his system, as both serving to educate the public and preserving the very structure of society. It was at least in its final realization, a vast propaganda device, designed to convince the working classes of the fundamental necessity of life's present inequalities and the need for cautious advancement in the future – a touchstone for what he saw as a rational and progressive society.

The essentially Victorian character of Pitt Rivers' vision stands out for us today. There is something both endearing and off-putting about his confidence in material progress, his aspirations for 'progress', his hopes for attaining an encyclopedic understanding of history through the comparison of mere objects. For Pitt Rivers, objects could not lie: they were determinate, undeniable 'facts' that, when put together, conveyed a sense of truth. Pitt Rivers' own personality, the 'persona' at least that has descended to us through his own writings and the accolades of his early chroniclers, adds a further dimension to that vision. In many ways, Pitt Rivers might be considered as emblematic of his time, a minor 'specimen' left out of Lytton Strachey's biographical portrait of the age. His most recent biographer, Michael Thompson, in fact treats him in just such a representative fashion, linking his work to that of other eminent Victorians, such as Darwin and Spencer, citing the Great Exhibition of 1851, that perennial symbol of mid-Victorian self-confidence and material self-satisfaction, as the point of departure for his collecting ideas (Thompson, 1977). But such a viewpoint fails to capture fully the complexity of the individual or to adequately trace Pitt Rivers' often shifting aims and expectations, particularly for his own collections. Pitt Rivers was in part a typical Victorian. His conventionalism, even in his apparent and often self-advertised idiosyncracies, is at times striking. But he also enjoyed a unique life, one subject to calamities, shifts in allegiance, one marked by a history of severe illness and often frustruated ambitions. Correspondingly, his ideas, especially his museum ideas, followed a similar course of intermittent adjustment and reappraisal, a course of development that has up to now been overlooked, or at least underplayed (van Keuren, 1984). For the sake of the record, it is worth breaking beneath the surface of received knowledge to examine his ideas in their more complete context.

Pitt Rivers and his early collection

Pitt Rivers, originally called Augustus Henry Lane Fox before a later inheritance required a change of name, was born in the north of England into a landed family closely tied to their Yorkshire estate and to affairs of country life. It was an unlikely environment for a future anthropologist, and furthermore, indications are that his early upbringing and training were fully in keeping with those of a young aristocrat of his time. At an early age he was sent to Sandhurst to pursue a military career – his older brother had chosen the diplomatic corps – but for a short time, after his own father's death, he was withdrawn from school and educated privately in London. At the age of eighteen he finally did enter the military, joining his father's former regiment, the Grenadier Guards, his commission purchased with the help of his wealthier relatives. (As the second son of a second son he had little money or expectations of his own, but he still had close ties to wealthy and well-connected people and would rely on those ties throughout his life, until his own inheritance many years later.) From 1845 until 1850 he performed typical military duty as a Lieutenant and then Captain in his regiment. In 1851, however, he was assigned to a new task as a musketry instructor, an assignment that was to have an important impact upon his career and his later museum ideas.

Pitt Rivers first began to collect objects of archaeological and ethnographical character around 1851 or 1852, or indeed shortly after the Great Exhibition of the Works of Art of All Nations held in Hyde Park. His first 'series', as he came to call the component divisions of his collection, was of early firearms, an interest stemming directly from his work as a musketry officer, first at Hythe and then at Woolwich, where he helped test and train troops in the use of the new rifles then being introduced into British service use. Evidently, this first collection was used for instruction. A pamphlet published in 1854 gives a hint of how such a collection was used to teach the history of arms to units under his charge (Pitt Rivers, 1854). A second collection formed at Hythe and apparently also begun by Pitt Rivers suggests an interesting parallel – even extending in time to 'primitive' weapons in addition to muskets and other European arms (Haddon, 1900). Pitt Rivers' core collection was soon supplemented by other arms, some antique and others what we would now consider as 'ethnographical', brought together to show the 'chain of progress' in the development of arms and the minute 'improvements' necessary for technological advance (1858). The broad outline of his collection is suggested by his later papers and, perhaps most revealingly, by other early books on the development of weapons to which he frequently referred.[3]

Throughout the 1850s Pitt Rivers gradually expanded his core collection largely through objects gathered by means of contacts in the military and as a result of his own travels. In 1855 he was sent to Malta in anticipation of the Crimean invasion and was assigned to further musketry instruction there. The war eventually took him to Turkey, the Crimea and modern Greece and Bulgaria, and there are examples of weapons, particularly swords, pikes, flails and so on, from each of those places in his collection.[4] Returning to London, again via Malta, in 1857, he shortly became active in the London Geographical Society to which he was nominated by the Assyriologist and explorer Henry Creswicke Rawlinson (1810–95), Roderick Impey Murchison (1792–1871), the Society's President, and his brother-in-law Henry Stanley (1827–1903).[5] He was also active at the United Services Institution, a forward-looking body located in Whitehall and dedicated to the 'fostering of knowledge' of military science among its members and the general public. Pitt Rivers, who was on half-pay at the time facing an inquiry into his training methods, spent much of his time at the Royal United Services Institution, where he presented several papers, served on a number of committees and apparently helped to reorganize the Institution's own collection.[6] It was an ideal situation for a collector, and Pitt Rivers acquired a number of pieces, and some of his earliest more complete collections, through contacts at the Institution. Among them were the large assortment of East African pieces collected by John Petherick (1813–82) and the Arctic collection of Admiral Edward Belcher (1799–1877), an acquaintance of Pitt Rivers since his days at Woolwich when Belcher was involved in developing a modern harpoon based on Eskimo examples for the British navy.[7] Pitt Rivers also frequented galleries and auction houses, and it is clear from auctioneers' records that at least by the early 1860s he had begun to collect objects other than weapons, including his early series on house types and a series on art and design.[8]

The late 1850s and early 1860s were overall a period of re-evaluation for Pitt Rivers. His military career, because of differences of opinion with his superiors, had come to a standstill. In fact, there was a very real possibility that the inquiry he faced might lead to a court martial. It is obvious from his family's correspondence that he saw himself as ill-used and undervalued, and that for him it was the military, not his own goals that needed reform. For Pitt Rivers the reaction took the form of a greater commitment to 'science' and a greater interest in scientific organizations, for him an alternative to what he saw as the moribund traditionalism of the services. Largely through his wife's relatives, the well-known Stanleys of Alderley Hall in Cheshire, he was introduced to scientific collectors such as Philip de Malpas Grey-Egerton (1806–81), a noted amateur naturalist, and Richard Owen (1804–92) then of the Hunterian Museum and later Director of the British Museum's Natural History Collections. He was also introduced to scientific societies, including the Royal Institution, made famous by Faraday's popular exhibitions of chemistry during the 1830s and 1840s. His father-in-law was Sir Edward John Stanley (1802–69), a powerful Liberal politician, one-time Postmaster General and President of the Board of Trade, and through Stanley Pitt Rivers became active on the committee for organizing the military exhibit at the International Exhibition of 1862.[9]

Pitt Rivers' scientific associations were matched by his readings. Again, largely through the Stanleys' influence, he undertook a programme of personal study in science and philosophy. His writings a few years later are sprinkled with references to Locke and Hume, Comte (at least Martineau's Comte), Spencer and Mills. Spencer and Mills were also visitors to the Stanley house, and it is likely that Pitt Rivers met them there. While his work was looked upon often sardonically by his clearly more sophisticated in-laws – 'Augustus is very full of Plato just now and likes it so much. . . . I never knew anyone put his ideas and principles so little into practice', quipped his sister-in-law Kate Stanley[10] – it is clear that Pitt Rivers was recasting himself as the knowledgeable scientific amateur, a person familiar with the progress of society and clearly committed to acquiring a scientific or 'objective' understanding of the world. His collection and collecting interests were inevitably coloured by his new involvement and by his changing self-conception. Publication of Darwin's *Origin of Species* in late 1859, an event that marked the scientific conversion of many, merely reassured Pitt Rivers that he was on the right track.

Assignment to Ireland and his early archaeological and ethnological work

In 1861 Pitt Rivers, having finally been exonerated, returned to active service, accompanying his regiment first to Canada, where he apparently acquired a number of north American pieces for his collection, and later being assigned to the post of Assistant Quarter-Master General for the south-west district in Ireland located in Cork. His position required that he remove himself and his growing family from London, and by necessity many of his scientific ties and associations were curtailed. He evidently subscribed to professional journals, including that of the Ethnological Society of London, which he joined in 1861, and also became active at the Cork Royal Institution and various local archaeological or antiquarian societies in Ireland, most importantly the Kilkenny and Southeast Ireland Archaeological Society (later the Royal Archaeological Society of Ireland).[11] It was during the time of his posting in Ireland that Pitt Rivers' archaeological interests first became apparent, although there are hints in his writings that he was at least intermittently involved in amateur excavations as early as the 1850s, largely as an outgrowth of his collecting interests.[12] In the early to mid-1860s he observed and participated in a number of small digs, devoting most of his time, however, to recording field remains with a fellow collector named Richard Caulfield (*d.*1887). His findings were described in *The Gentleman's Magazine* and later in the *Archaeological Journal*, the main journal of the Archaeological Institute to which he was nominated by his wife's uncle Albert Way (1805–74) in 1864 (Caulfield, 1865; Pitt Rivers, 1867c).[13] He was also elected to the prestigious Society of Antiquaries of London beginning in 1863, mostly for his work on 'ancient arms and armour', again being supported by Albert Way and the ethnographer Henry Christy (1810–65), along with a close friend and fellow arms collector from the Royal United Services Institution, Arthur Tupper.[14] As a result of his work in Ireland, his collection became increasingly 'archaeo-logical' in character, although, of course, in broad outline it could be said to have been at least 'antiquarian' in intent from the beginning, a point stressed in Pitt Rivers' own papers of the 1860s. Pitt Rivers also established ties with the British Museum's Department of British and Medieval Antiquities and Ethnography, presenting a collection of Ogham-inscribed stones to the collection in 1864 and working out particulars of shipment, etc. with the then chief of the department, Augustus Wollaston Franks (1826–97).[15]

One of the main byproducts of Pitt Rivers' stay in Ireland was a harshening of his racial views. Pitt Rivers, like many others of the time, had shown an interest in races and the idea of racial development from an early period. Partly this was the result of his exposure to different peoples during his travels, partly a result of his readings, especially about the peoples who had manufactured the weapons represented in his collection. For Pitt Rivers, as with others, there was a certain amount of overlap in thinking about the nature of individual development and that of whole races. Drawing particularly upon the work of the phrenologist Charles Bray (1811–84), Pitt Rivers conceived of various races as representing different stages in the development of mankind overall, or of European civilization, and also as corresponding to different phases in the maturation of an individual, from infancy, through childhood and adulthood.[16] 'Savage races', as he observed, were representative of humanity in its infancy, much as 'savage' weapons represented those produced at an early stage in the history of human technological development (Pitt Rivers, 1867b). This persistent equation of mental development and technological advancement was certainly not peculiar to Pitt Rivers, and in fact was a fairly common understanding among ethnologists and incipient 'psychologists' of the period, but it was to become a peculiar hallmark of his collecting ideas (see, for example, Crawfurd, 1862, 1864; Knox, 1862a, 1862b). Not only were savage peoples the manufacturers of simple or primitive instruments – but it was *all* they were mentally capable of producing.

In Ireland, Pitt Rivers' racial views coloured his perception of the Irish people. When called upon in 1866 to serve as the prosecuting officer in the case of three Fenian 'conspirators' in one of the south-west regiments – an assignment that incidently gave him coverage and a picture in the *London Illustrated News*[17] – Pitt Rivers saw the problem as 'racial' and not 'political' in character. 'Fenianism', he explained, '[is] a war of races indeed' and is to be found in 'the social ethical and the psichological (sic) condition of the people'.[18] Such a view, coupled with an almost peculiarly militaristic reading of Darwin, was to have a strong effect upon the formal development of Pitt Rivers' ideas, at least for a number of years.

Pitt Rivers returned to London from Ireland, initially in 1865 and permanently in 1866, or around the time of the Fenian Trial. In 1867, he again went officially on half-pay, apparently for reasons of ill-health. (He was later diagnosed as a diabetic and his bouts with the disease appear to have been periodic.) Pitt Rivers again used his free time to good effect, working on various papers describing both his collection and his recent archaeological work, as well as undertaking fresh surveys and excavations, first in the Thames Valley, where he compared his discovery of flint chips *in situ* to the famous work of Boucher de Perthes in the Somme Valley, and later with Canon William Greenwell (1820–18), a pioneering field archaeologist introduced to Pitt Rivers by Albert Way, in the Yorkshire Wolds (Pitt Rivers, 1866a, 1866b, 1867a, 1867b, 1869a, 1869b, 1882a, 1882b).[19] He also became active again in scientific and archaeological organizations, from which he had been cut off for several years, and renewed his involvement in the United Services Institution.

The state of his collection during those years can only be known in outline form, although it is clear that it had attained immense proportions, far outstripping the typical assemblage of natural history specimens or artistic objects that embellished the homes of many of his contemporaries. E.B. Tylor, who knew Pitt Rivers during this period, recorded that the collection reached from the basement to the attic of his house, then at 10 Phillimore Gardens, Kensington (1917), and it is clear that Pitt Rivers conceived of it as a fully 'scientific' collection, with all that it entailed in terms of explanatory charts, labels and display cases. Unfortunately, other than lists set out in his published papers, no catalogue was made of the collection as it stood then, so that much of the history of its growth and the development of its series can only be reconstructed in a fragmentary way.[20] We know, however, that by the late 1860s it included a number of series of weapons and related items, such as bows and arrows, spears, pikes and body armour as well as series showing the evolution of ornamental design, the development of weaving, basketry and pottery, one on 'superstition' and human representation and another illustrating the supposed transition of clubs to canoe paddles, perhaps one of the more ambitious series in his collection. There was also a small series of skulls, casts of skulls and other anatomical specimens, including several examples of skulls from Ireland (compared in this instance to those of New Guinea), although this aspect of the collection was never fully developed as Pitt Rivers himself admitted, later referring visitors to more specialist collections for information.[21] Still, the connection between racial development and technological development remained an implicit message, especially during this period.

Two major influences upon Pitt Rivers' collection during the 1860s and upon his ideas for museums were the collections of the Royal Irish Academy in Dublin, recently reorganized and catalogued by Sir

William Robert Wills Wilde (1815–76), father, incidentally, of Oscar, and of Henry Christy, a London collector, antiquarian and ethnographer. Whether Pitt Rivers visited or corresponded with Wilde during his stay in Ireland is unclear. It is certain, however, that he was aware of Wilde's reorganization of the Academy's materials along lines similar to his own, referring to Wilde's catalogue frequently in the course of his own writing and modelling copies in his collection directly on those in the Academy and illustrated in Wilde's books (see Pitt Rivers, 1865, 1867b: 636, 645; Wilde 1857–62). But the main connection was the idea of scientific principles. Wilde argued in his several catalogues of the Academy's mostly archaeological materials, that antiquities could be organized according to various 'classes', 'orders' and 'species' along the lines of natural history collections. Such a scheme had been propounded in the past, most importantly by the French geographer and ethnographer, Esme-Françoise Jomard (1777–1862), and it is possible that Pitt Rivers knew of Jomard's proposal as well.[22] But it was still to Wilde's system that Pitt Rivers most closely compared his own and indeed, which really because of its archaeological emphasis, most closely approximated his own in intent.

Henry Christy's collection on the other hand took another direction in its method of organization and, in fact, was arranged strictly on the basis of geographical origin, as had been proposed by the first truly systematic champion of ethnographical or ethnological collections, Phillip Franz Balthazar von Siebold (1796–1866), whose own argument for a geographical system in the 1830s and 1840s had been widely publicized and known, including by Pitt Rivers who referred to a number of Siebold's publications.[23] Christy's collection, which was housed in his apartment on Victoria Street, had been bequeathed to the nation upon his death in 1865 and was administered after that date by the British Museum's Department of British and Medieval Antiquities and Ethnography and more specifically by Pitt Rivers' acquaintance, Wollaston Franks. Franks, in fact, paid for the cost of the custodian, Charles Hercules Read (1857–1929), later the curator of the ethnographical collections, out of his own pocket. Pitt Rivers was familiar with the collection both before and after Christy's death, even contributing a number of pieces to the collection over the years;[24] Christy, it will be remembered, had also been one of Pitt Rivers' sponsors at the Society of Antiquarians and was probably the main collector of ethnographical objects in Britain at the time – and, incidentally, a frequent bidder at many of the same auctions Pitt Rivers had attended.[25] Overall, Pitt Rivers tended to contrast his system to that of Christy, arguing that Christy had adopted a more conventional system.[26] Still, Christy had a number of series similar to those of Pitt Rivers and had also been intent upon drawing similar connections between ethnographical and archaeological materials. With Christy's death, however, the future of the collection, at least of the collection as the product of a single scheme, was uncertain. It was left for Pitt Rivers to continue Christy's efforts – and also, to find a focus for them.

The Ethnological and Anthropological Societies and Pitt Rivers' papers of the 1860s

During this period, or the years between 1865 and 1869, Pitt Rivers' attention, and his efforts on behalf of his collection, came increasingly to concentrate on two organizations: the Ethnological Society of London, an organization that he had joined in 1861 just prior to his departure for Ireland, and the Anthropological Society, a relatively new organization founded only in 1863, that Pitt Rivers joined in 1865 during a return visit home.[27] Both organizations were important to the development of Pitt Rivers' ideas, and helped him both to frame and promote his theories, particularly his theories on the evolution of tehnology, in a wider context than that allowed for by such special-interest bodies as the Royal United Services Institution. Also, both societies were young and open to change and new ideas. The Ethnological Society of London had been founded in 1843 but had been effectively reformed and reconstituted in the early 1860s; the Anthropological Society was new altogether. This meant that Pitt Rivers had a great opportunity for making an impact and for making his collection both known and somehow relevant to the issues at hand, especially when compared to his opportunities in the more conservative and established Archaeological Institute or Society of Antiquaries where Pitt Rivers was a relative newcomer despite his family connections. It is really only through reference to the Ethnological and Anthropological Societies and the debates surrounding both their formation and what might be considered their 'methodologies' that full relevance of Pitt Rivers initiatives and aims for his collection became apparent.

The Ethnological and Anthropological Societies were at the same time both kindred organizations and competitors. The Ethnological Society had a longer pedigree and could trace itself to the Quaker-dominated Aborigines Protection Society of the 1830s (see, for example, Burrow, 1963, 1966; Stocking, 1971). While the organization had suffered numerous vicissitudes during its history, and by the late 1850s had lost most of its membership, it was still permeated by a spirit of open inquiry and by the solicitous concern for the conditions of aboriginal peoples first instilled in it by early members such as James Cowles Prichard (1786–1848), Thomas Hodgkin (1798–1866) and Robert Gordon Latham (1812–88). During the early 1860s this spirit was resuscitated by newer members such as Thomas Huxley (1825–95), John Lubbock (1834–1913) and John Evans (1823–1908), all of whom retained an essentially 'liberal' and protective attitude towards the actual subjects of their inquiry. The Anthropological Society had been formed largely in opposition to those principles, espousing a programme based not on what they considered charity, but on cold 'facts' and scientific evidence. Founded by breakaway members of the Ethnological Society, principally James Hunt (1833–69) and his followers, Thomas Bendyshe, Dean Frederick Farrar (1831–1903) and most famously, the African explorer, Richard Burton (1821–1900) the Anthropological Society was in many ways as much a racialist club – its meetings, for example, were called to order by a gavel in the shape of a Negro's head – as a serious scientific organization, although its message was always couched in the strictest terms of 'objectivity' (Hunt, 1863a). Both societies, however, professed to scientific truthfulness and both were caught up in many of the same debates.

The main concern of both organizations, particularly during Pitt Rivers' early years of involvement, was the question of the 'monogenesis' or 'polygenesis' of man, briefly put, the question of whether human races had a single origin or a multiple one. James Cowles Prichard had seen the issue in moral terms: if other races were 'not our fellow creatures', he wrote in 1843, 'our relations with these tribes will appear to be not very different from those that might be imagined to subsist between us and a race of orangs' (Lienhardt, 1964). Much of his work, and that of other Society members, was dedicated to reconstructing what might be called the pre-history of man, mostly through the comparison of languages, or 'historical philogy', as it was termed, and by this means to establish a time and place of origin – generally assumed to total about 30,000 years and to have been somewhere in central Asia. Hunt and his followers, on the other hand, were intent upon disproving Prichard's theories. They pointed to the vast length of time involved, particularly after the recent revelations by archaeologists that man had existed far longer than previously supposed. Hunt estimated the time at 'millions' of years and also stressed that the vast discrepancies, both physical and mental, among the world's present races appeared to be of long duration as well (Hunt, 1863b: 6; Grayson, 1983; Crawfurd, 1862). (One main piece of evidence was skulls and skull types, a particular interest to the anthropologists.) At the time of Pitt Rivers' involvement these issues were still fresh and – a point that has not been sufficiently stressed in previous histories of the field (Stocking, 1971) – lay at the very heart of the rejuvenated interest in ethnological questions during that period. Pitt Rivers with his collection of enthropological and archaeological materials was in what he saw as the ideal position to make an original contribution to the debate.

Pitt Rivers' response took the form of a series of three papers presented at the Royal United Services Institution annually between 1867 and 1869. They were intended for a general audience but obviously were directed primarily at the ethnological and anthropological communities. In his papers, he presents his basic ideas on the evolution of technology. 'Weapons', as he explained, developed from the natural forms: antlers were converted to jabbing implements, horns to spear points and so on. Technological development corresponded generally to mental development. Drawing again upon the work of Bray, he compared 'savages' to children, more advanced peoples – 'the semi-civilized' – to adolescents. The ability to either transfer or independently develop technology was contingent upon mental abilities, as again determined by race. The ideal of 'invention' itself was suspect. Most advances were made as a result as slow, almost imperceptible improvement, revealing Pitt Rivers' fundamental adherance to a uniformitarian viewpoint, and through the transfer of technology from one race to another. Indicative of Pitt Rivers' membership in the Anthropological Society, certain races, of which the primary example was the modern European, were the beneficiaries of the progress developments of man, a circumstance in large part attributed to racially determined capabilities. It was, as he explained, the destiny of some races to conquer and destroy others, and, he stressed, 'the mere fact of one race supplanting another proves its superiority' (Pitt Rivers, 1867b: 619).

In a parallel sense, similar arguments were developed for the 'evolution' of stone and bronze tools, one tool 'succeeding' another almost as once race replaced that inferior to it. Appropriating the phraseology of the ethnological and anthropological debate, the question of the 'monogenesis' or 'polygenesis' of bronze tools was discussed in depth, particularly in his third paper; differences or similarities in character among tools were attributed to differences or similarities in the raw materials and methods of manufacture. Throughout, the emphasis was on the links between different techniques and the imperceptible shifts in function from stick to shield or from club to paddle and, overall, the continuous nature of technological advance (or correspondingly in some instances, 'decay' or 'degeneration' of forms). The process was compared to a branching tree – here the reference to Darwin is explicit – with each branch representing separated developments and adaptations (Plates 2, 3).

The image of a branching tree was, in fact, of primary importance to Pitt Rivers' scheme, recalling, as it did, the ethnological debate on origins. If mere 'words', or rather the comparative study of languages, had failed to trace mankind back to his several or a single origins, artefacts could serve that function better. For one, objects were reliable; 'artefacts cannot intentionally mislead us', Pitt Rivers pronounced (1869b). Second, they could be used to extend man's history back to the more remote times, in accordance with the newly understood archaeological record. Exactly how they could be used was developed in detail in the last part of his second and in his third lecture. Referring to a recent paper of Huxley's on the origin and distribution of the 'Austroloid' race, Pitt Rivers demonstrated a continuity among artefacts, particularly throwing sticks, among the peoples of south India, east Africa and Australia, all of which were considered by Huxley to have been formed from a single root on the basis of such traditional ethnological (as opposed to anthropological) criteria as skin colour and hair type (Huxley, 1869, 1870). Similarities in tool assemblages, Pitt Rivers stressed, allowed for historical reconstruction beyond that offered by physiological evidence, helping to trace the race to its origins. It would only be necessary to fill in the record more completely, first through the collection of more objects and eventually through a more detailed knowledge of the geological history of the region in order to know the details of origins and distribution (1869b: 516, 1874b: 618). For Pitt Rivers, the

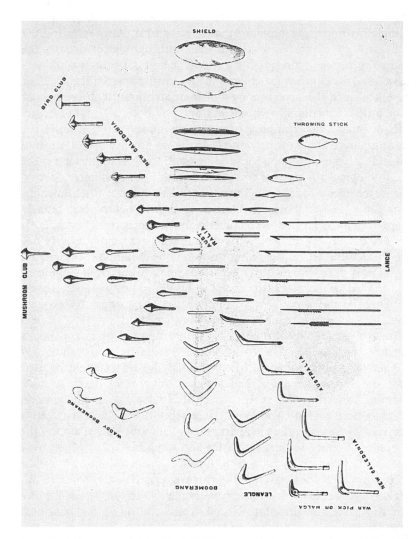

Plate 2   Diagram published by Pitt Rivers in his paper 'On the evolution of
culture' in *Journal of the Anthropological Institute* 7, 1875: 357–89.
It demonstrates the evolution of a number of weapons and
implements from an original 'core' invention – the common stick.
Photograph: author courtesy of Royal Anthropological Institute.

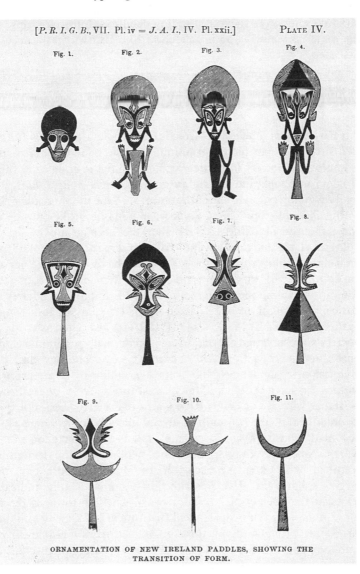

[*P. R. I. G. B.*, VII. Pl. iv = *J. A. I.*, IV. Pl. xxii.]   PLATE IV.

Fig. 1.   Fig. 2.   Fig. 3.   Fig. 4.

Fig. 5.   Fig. 6.   Fig. 7.   Fig. 8.

Fig. 9.   Fig. 10.   Fig. 11.

ORNAMENTATION OF NEW IRELAND PADDLES, SHOWING THE
TRANSITION OF FORM.

Plate 3   Diagram published by Pitt Rivers in his paper 'On the evolution of culture' in *Journal of the Anthropological Institute* 7, 1875: 375–89. The origin of ornamental design was a common preoccupation of the mid-Victorians, Pitt Rivers among them. Photograph: author courtesy of Royal Anthropological Institute.

ultimate solution to the longstanding debate on human origins lay in the material record – and a collection like his own was a necessary first step.

The collection in a public context

Pitt Rivers spent much of his free time during the late 1860s and early 1870s trying to put his programme into effect. He was active at the Ethnological Society in particular, his loyalties to colleagues such as Huxley, Lubbock and the fellow archaeologist John Evans, eventually winning out over the earlier appeal of the more racialist clique within the Anthropological Society; in 1868 he broke entirely with what George Stocking has labelled the core group of 'anthropologicals', turning down Hunt's offer to serve as president of the by then clearly failing organization.[28] In 1868 he served on the negotiating committee for amalgamation and also served on various special committees within the again reconstituted Ethnological Society; new governing regulations were drawn up in 1868 largely following the outline suggested by Pitt Rivers.[29] Pitt Rivers also acted as head of the Society's archaeological committee and drew up preliminary guidelines for the collection and recording of technology and other material arts, guidelines that were eventually to be incorporated within the later Anthropological Institute's *Notes and Queries*.[30] Together with Huxley, Pitt Rivers also organized a series of special exhibits held at the Museum of Economic Geology (where Huxley had held a position) in the spring of 1869.[31] Subjects included the North American Indians and the peoples of the Indian subcontinent – the latter the occasion for Huxley's address on racial origins.[32] Later Pitt Rivers worked on a similar lecture and exhibit series at the Society of Antiquaries. In working towards the final formation of the Anthropological Institute in 1871, an eventuality in large part brought about through the efforts of Huxley, Evans, Lubbock and Pitt Rivers himself, Pitt Rivers attempted to ensure a central place for the study of technology and material culture, through explicit supporting links with the British Museum (stressed in a paper at the British Association meeting in Brighton in 1872) and through a well-defined programme for collecting and recording, set out in *Notes and Queries* in 1873 (Pitt Rivers, 1872a; Urry, 1972; see also Pitt Rivers, 1872b, 1872c). (Pitt Rivers, incidentally, also paid for the cost of the first edition himself.) Still, it was apparent that most other anthropologists, while not opposed to his ideas, were not adopting them with the enthusiasm with which he might have wished. Even at this early date it was clear that the study of material culture was going to be peripheral to the main anthropological programme.

Pitt Rivers, perhaps in part because of the lack of enthusiasm on the part of his colleagues, increasingly oriented his efforts towards the general public. In several ways, of course, his collection had had broadly pedagogical purposes from the beginning, when he used it for the education of troops. During the 1870s, however, the educational possibilities of his collection became further defined, largely as a result of his experience with temporary exhibits and also in response to a more general recognition of the educational potential for museums in the popular and scientific journals. As early as 1864, for example, John Edward Gray (1800–75) of the British Museum's Zoological Department had stressed the need of good public museums, dedicated to the 'diffusion of instruction . . . and amusement among the mass of people', an argument pressed even earlier by Edward Forbes (1815–54) of the Museum of Economic Geology and his then assistant Thomas Huxley as well (Gray, 1864; Forbes, 1853, 1854; Huxley, 1865, 1866). By the early 1870s, in fact, popular education through museums had become something of a national cause, reflected in Parliamentary debates on the management of the British Museum and in the efforts for new both national and local collections (Greenwood, 1888). While the need for continuing research and for professional supervision were accepted premises, the main emphasis of museums was to shift entirely.

Pitt Rivers was drawn inevitably into the new museum movement during the 1870s and indeed in many ways saw himself as one of the main progenitors of the cause. In 1872 he loaned a number of musical instruments from his collection for a special exhibit at South Kensington;[33] and in 1874 he finally arranged with the South Kensington authorities, specifically the Science and Art Department, to place his whole collection temporarily in the new South Kensington branch museum at Bethnal Green (Plates 4, 5). Located in the heart of London's East End – Bethnal Green had been singled out by publicists of the period as the worst example of urban poverty[34] – the branch museum was specifically intended to help 'improve' the masses through educational exhibits. Other exhibits of the early 1870s, or the period immediately after completion of the building known as the Brompton

Plate 4   Old weavers houses, Bethnal Green, the setting for Pitt Rivers' first public display of his collection. His museum was intended to help this sector of society understand its place in the universal 'progress'. From *Pictorial London: Views of the Streets , Public Buildings , Parks and Scenes of the Metropolis* (Cassell and Co.: London, 1906): 260. Photograph: author.

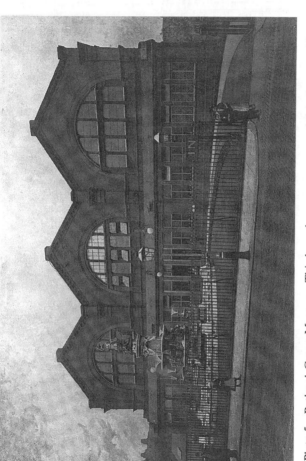

Plate 5   Bethnal Green Museum. This branch museum was established to provide an educational outlet for the South Kensington Museum in the early 1870s. The The Pitt Rivers collection was displayed here in 1874, when it was transferred to the main museum. From *Pictorial London: Views of the Streets , Public Buildings , Parks and Scenes of the Metropolis* (Cassell and Co.: London, 1906): 260. Photograph: author.

Boilers (named after the metal superstructures left over from the International Exhibition of 1862) included a display of food and animal products, a demonstration of weaving technology – many of the inhabitants of the area were descendants of Huguenot weavers – and a special exhibit of paintings from the Wallace collection, arranged in strictly chronological order. Pitt Rivers' collection fit easily into this context, and was displayed in two semi-basement rooms along the north side. Labels and new cases were provided and arrows were placed strategically to direct visitors through the exhibit. Pitt Rivers also provided a lengthy, though still incomplete, catalogue. The display was opened in the summer of 1874, and the occasion was celebrated by a special meeting of the Anthropological Institute. Following his own lecture on the 'Principles of classification', Pitt Rivers lead members through the maze of display cases, including by that time over 10,000 separate pieces, and pointed out objects of particular interest.[35] The whole event was well received by the anthropological community, but the impression is of polite recognition rather than enthusiasm. For the next four years the collection was to remain at Bethnel Green, an object of some interest to residents as attendance records suggest, but relatively neglected by the anthropological community.[36]

One of the main reasons that Pitt Rivers had placed his collection on display, other than the fact that he clearly wished to publicize it and make it useful, was that he was at the time re-entering the army to serve as head of the Brigade Depot in Guildford. This required that he close his home and move his family, by then including nine children, out of London. While the collection remained on public display – after 1878 at the main gallery in South Kensington – Pitt Rivers dedicated his time to other pursuits. Among his publications of the period were two papers on the physiological characteristics of troops and a number of archaeological papers (1874c, 1874a, 1877). It was also during this period that Pitt Rivers undertook his well-known series of excavations of Iron Age hill forts, collaborating with George Rolleston (1829–81) at Cissbury for a second campaign in 1874–75 (Pitt Rivers, 1875b, 1868, 1880). His efforts on behalf of his collection were cursory: one paper on 'primitive navigation' published in 1874 and obviously written before his departure to Guildford and a second entitlted 'The evolution of culture', essentially a recapitulation of his ideas in 'Principles of Classification', but with a stronger 'Spencerian' rather than 'Darwinian' emphasis with its stress on the idea of transition from 'simplicity' to 'complexity' and from 'homogeneous' to 'heterogenous' (Pitt Rivers, 1875a).

Part of the reason for his neglect of his collection was simply because he was away from London and forced to rely on materials at hand. But also, the problems of archaeology were themselves beginning to hold greater interest for him. In many ways, it was logical extension of his collecting interests, incorporating as it did the minutiae of stratigraphic evidence, rather than the record of 'surface distribution' as exemplified in his collection. Also, his collection was in reasonably secure hands, and, in a sense, could serve as its own advertisement.

By 1879, however, it was clear that something was going to have to be done in order to place his collection and his programme for the advancement of anthropology on a more permanent footing. Later that year he offered it formally to the nation with the understanding that it would remain at South Kensington, forming the nucleus of both a teaching institution for students of anthropology and a place of public instruction. The nation, in turn, as well as the several anthropologists and educators appointed to advise the Parliamentary Committee, had finally to consider the offer seriously.

Gift of the collection to Oxford

Pitt Rivers offered his collection to South Kensington in 1879, and in 1880 his offer was turned down. While Pitt Rivers attempted to influence the special committee appointed by Parliament to advise the governors of the museum (specifically the Lords of the Committee of Council on Education), writing directly to argue his case,[37] the final ruling was that Pitt Rivers' collection would be in conflict with that already housed at the British Museum, thus duplicating the nation's efforts on behalf of anthropology.[38] The other, less explicit issue was that of control over the collection: Pitt Rivers offered to pay the cost of a curator and custodian but insisted that he retain overall authority over the collection, including the right to add or subtract as many objects to or from the collection as he pleased, something the museum authorities were understandably reluctant to accept. Pitt Rivers, of course, was furious at the outcome. The British Museum, he had told Franks, was 'useless' for purposes of public education. As he threatened Franks, 'If I cannot get more space at South

Kensington . . . I shall build a museum in or close to London . . . [and] become a collector of ethnographical gems'.[39] Now that the Council on Education had made its decision, however, nothing more could be done. Pitt Rivers simply had to look elsewhere for a recipient for his collection or make good on his threat.

In the meantime, however, Pitt Rivers had other matters to tend to. Most importantly, in 1880, he had suddenly and unexpectedly come into his inheritance, an eventuality that transformed him from a well-connected, though at times impecunious, soldier on half-pay, to a wealthy man. In all the estate, previously belonging to his uncle on his mother's side, the 6th Lord Rivers, consisted of some 30,000 acres, on the border of Wiltshire and Dorset, a county seat called Farnham Hall, several secondary residences, including a thirteenth-century manor house traditionally thought to be a hunting lodge of King John's, and an impressive mansion at Grosvenor Gardens over-looking Buckingham Palace. The inheritance carried with it numer-ous responsibilities: the estate farms had to be overseen, and the welfare of two agricultural villages had to be attended to; Pitt Rivers, an affirmed 'agnostic', even had control over two parishes and two livings.

The estate also offered numerous opportunities for archaeological fieldwork, and almost immediately upon taking possession of the property he began the series of famous excavations that eventually was to secure his reputation as the founder of modern archaeology. For the first time also he had near-unlimited resources with which to carry out his work. He was able to hire assistants and draftsmen and to offer employment to as many as thirty full-time laborers – paid an extra shilling a week over what they made during the summer working on his estate. But still, all was not ideal. Pitt Rivers throughout the time of his inheritance was severely ill, often carrying out his excavations from his sick bed with the help of his assistants. Soon to be diagnosed and treated through the adherence to a rigorous diet, Pitt Rivers' condition brought him close to death.[40] He obviously was concerned throughout this period to clear up his affairs. Disposal of his museum became increasingly a priority.

In 1882, John Obediah Westwood (1805–93), a close friend of Pitt Rivers' uncle Albert Way and the Hope Professor of Zoology at Oxford, was asked, apparently through intermediaries, if the Uni-versity would be interested in the collection. There was, of course, a long-standing tradition of giving collections to the university;

Oxford's first collection, which, in turn, formed a nucleus of the Ashmolean Museum, had been the result of a single gift, and in many ways Pitt Rivers' decision followed the traditional pattern of aristocratic patronage. Also, George Rolleston, Pitt Rivers' closest friend and archaeological collaborator, had held a position at Oxford. His death in 1881 had come as a shock, and it is apparent that Pitt Rivers considered his gift as in some ways a memorial to Rolleston as well.[42] The terms were similar to those offered the South Kensington Museum, but in this case Pitt Rivers was willing, for the first time – at least on paper – to relinquish some of his control. Also the provision to provide a curator and lecturer was deleted; the university was expected to fill both positions for its part in the transaction.[43] In 1883 the offer was formally approved by the university, and beginning in 1885, the collection, by then numbering some 14,000 items, was packed and removed to Oxford where it awaited the completion of a new building to house it (essentially a wing attached to the University's Science Museum). E.B. Tylor was appointed to the position of Reader (he also held the university post of Keeper of the Museum to make up the much-needed difference in his salary) and Henry Moseley, a biologist and ethnographer best known for his work as part of the 'Challenger' expedition – and also Rolleston's successor as Linacre Professor of Comparative Anatomy – undertook the task of overseeing the transfer of the collection from London. Young Walter Baldwin Spencer (1860–1929), later famous for his work on Australian kinship systems, and Henry Balfour (1863–1939) were hired to do the actual work. By 1887, most of the collection had been unpacked and arranged in cases and on display boards, and later in the year a large part of it was finally opened to the public.[44] Whether Pitt Rivers understood the full implications of his gift or not, anthropology had finally found a place in the university.

Throughout the period of the collection's transfer and establishment at Oxford, Pitt Rivers had occupied himself primarily with his estate and with his own excavations. Publication of his findings, presented in the first of his lavishly produced volumes called *Excavations in Cranborne Chase*, began only in 1887, but his time between his inheritance and actual publication was taken up largely with the work itself. He had little to do with Oxford, other than answering occasional letters of inquiry from Balfour, who had in the meantime been assigned curatorial responsibilities, first as Moseley's assistant and eventually as full curator. A visit by Pitt Rivers to

Plate 6 Upper Gallery, Pitt Rivers Museum *c*1890. Henry Balfour, the Assistant Curator, is shown in the upper gallery of the collection; the collection was opened to the public soon afterwards. Photograph: courtesy of the Pitt Rivers Museum, Oxford.

Plate 7 Interior of Pitt Rivers Museum, Oxford, photographed by Alfred Robinson, *c* 1899. Edward Burnett Tylor's totem pole had just been erected. Photograph: courtesy of the Pitt Rivers Museum, Oxford.

Oxford in 1888, however, disturbed him, largely because the work was coming so slowly. When Balfour published some of his own findings (or speculations) 'On the structure and affinities of the composite bow' (1889) Pitt Rivers' disenchantment with Oxford and his own decision came to a head. Balfour was informed that he was not to publish anything more on the collection until Pitt Rivers was 'done' with it.[45] In the meantime, he was to continue the work of setting the collection up and managing the system that Pitt Rivers himself had invented. Circumstances clearly did not provide a climate for further research – research of a kind originally called for by Pitt Rivers – and one wonders, in fact, if Pitt Rivers ever fully understood what true, open-minded research entailed. But then too, Pit Rivers' own programme for the collection had drifted almost imperceptibly away from research towards popular education. Oxford and he were simply not of one mind (Plates 6, 7).

In the meantime, partly as a result of circumstances at Oxford and partly because of his new interests, Pitt Rivers began a second collection of his own – in some ways fulfilling his earlier threat. Beginning with archaeological specimens and models, be soon extended his new 'series' to include examples of ethnographic and folk implements, agricultural tools and works of art that he thought would be of interest to 'the rural population 10 miles distant from any town or railway station'. A vacant school house, once used for the education of gypsy children on his estate, was appropriated for the museum, and by the early 1890s the collection was open to the public on a regular basis. To attract visitors, Pitt Rivers eventually added a small menagerie (really a game park not unlike those at a number of Britain's present stately homes), a picture gallery, picnic tables and shelters, refreshment stands and, on Sundays, a band composed of members at his agricultural workforce. The museum itself – modelled in part on Arthus Hazelius' folk museum outside Stockholm[46] – followed his earlier scheme as closely as possible: objects were arranged by category and the whole was organized to inculcate in the viewer 'an appreciation for the slow growth and stability of human institutions and industries' (Pitt Rivers, 1888: 823). Although relatively isolated, the museum received a fairly large number of visitors. Some days, in fact, entry figures totalled in the hundreds (Pitt Rivers, 1882a: xviii). A small hotel was even provided for visitors from greater distances. While far from attaining his earlier vision of a great anthropological collection organized by the nation, a topic returned to in his address before the British Association in 1888, by the mid-1890s, Pitt Rivers had fulfilled many of his ambitions in founding what he considered to be a truly popular museum.

If Pitt Rivers' efforts by this period appear to have had an even more explicit political bias than before, this is because they did. An affirmed Liberal during the 1850s and 1860s, Pitt Rivers gradually drifted towards conservatism and ultimately the Conservative Party, finally breaking with the Liberals, like so many others, over the issue of Home Rule for Ireland.[47] Pitt Rivers' shift in orientation also reflected the change in his circumstances: he was older, and he was no longer an unmonied professional soldier but a wealthy aristocrat with vast resources under his control. Conditions of the time also helped create a conservative reaction. The late 1870s had been a period of agricultural depression, initiated through repeal of protective Corn Laws and competitive foreign grain. The economic slump had resulted in both rural and urban unrest and was marked by a series of strikes and clashes with the authorities (see Perry, 1973; Richter, 1981). For Pitt Rivers any means possible to convince 'the masses' of the need for orderliness and patience was to be commended. Entering politics himself as a candidate for county office in 1888, he argued that the future lay not with politics, but with 'scientific men': 'We should listen to what they have to tell us when they treat upon social evolution, as they see the affairs of the world from a much higher standpoint than political men who are merely wire pullers and partisans'.[48] While Pitt Rivers lost the campaign – the suggestion that he was an 'atheist' and follower of Darwin did little to win sympathy among the many church-going voters in his district[49] – he had managed in many ways to change the emphasis of his earlier ideas, including his ideas on museums and education. Rather than stressing the need for research and open-minded investigation, Pitt Rivers now called for the reiteration of a kind of evolutionary catechism. All new material and fresh discovery were simply new grist for his pedagogical mill.

Pitt Rivers continued with his work throughout the last decade of his life – or the last decade of the century. His museum grew, including the addition of the well-known Benin bronzes in 1897, and visitors continued to be attracted to this at once both eccentric and original attraction (Pitt Rivers, 1900). His field work progressed at even greater speed and by the time of his death in 1900, four volumes had been published and a fifth begun; a separate fifth volume was

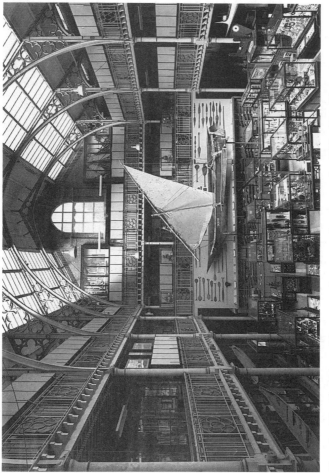

Plate 8   The Pitt Rivers Museum as it appeared as late as the 1970s. This Victorian collection has since been re-housed in more modern exhibition galleries. Photograph: courtesy of the Pitt Rivers Museum, Oxford.

Plate 9 'The Anthropological Rotunda' – the 1960s proposal f or a new Pitt Rivers Museu in Oxford. This grand scheme was never built. Photograph: courtesy of the Pitt Rivers Museum, Oxford.

published shortly afterwards by his assistant Harold St George Gray. It was overall an impressive life's work and one with which Pitt Rivers could be justly proud. Still, his lack of success in putting forward his museum ideas continued to rankle. In the last year of his life he complained bitterly to F.W. Rudler, then President of the Royal Anthropological Institute:

> Oxford was not the place for it and I should never have given it there if I had not been ill at the time and anxious to find a resting place for [my collection] of some kind in the future. I have always regretted it, and my new museum at Farnham, Dorset, represents my views on the subject much better.[50]

But beyond that nothing more was to be done. Anthropology had found a place in the university, but the system itself had shifted in its emphasis. The 'typological museum' idea had become transformed but at the same time somehow had lost much of its original thrust in the process.

Conclusions

It is tempting when reflecting upon the history of Pitt Rivers' museum ideas and of his collections, to suggest that Pitt Rivers' own often outspoken support did perhaps more to defeat the idea of a museum-based anthropology during his lifetime than to help. In many ways Pitt Rivers, through the force of his personality, his wealth and influence, managed almost to make the whole field his own. Independent research, such as that carried out by Balfour, was quashed whenever it occurred, and the impression is that anyone writing on material culture within the anthropological community was considered as somehow stepping on Pitt Rivers' turf. Also, as his ideas became more rigid, and his 'system' more propagandistic than instructive or open-ended, there was less room, at least in his mind, for research of any other kind – something that came out in particular in his relations with Oxford. Anthropology itself, following the sudden burst of interest among the public during the 1860s, had lapsed in popularity, a fact that more 'historicist' treatments of the subject tend to overlook. The advent of what is now recognized as 'evolutionism' in the 1870s had introduced a period, in Kuhn's terms, of normal science. But there was little growth in the field – the number of amateur anthropologists in fact decreased – and few fresh ideas. Neither the British Museum nor Oxford nor any of the other larger anthropological collections managed to create a 'school' of material culture on par with those in Germany or Scandinavia or even the United States. Most anthropologists of the time turned to other subjects altogether, particularly religion and what might broadly be called 'psychology' and 'sociology', all within the general framework of 'evolutionism'.

In the early twentieth century, anthropology was to shift again – this time, as is well known, towards field research – leading in turn to the contextural investigation of social structures and the study of kinship. This, of course, was the great structural-functionalist or *social* anthropological revolution of the teens and twenties, the origins of which can be traced by the Cambridge Torres Straits expedition of the 1890s, and it is really from this period that the history of modern British anthropology with its roots in the university – and the Colonial Office – truly begins. There remained 'museum men' (and women) and musem-oriented anthropologists, but they were few in number and were concerned primarily with issues such as admission policies, methods of display and the education of school groups rather than research of the type at one time proposed by Pitt Rivers. (Even where Pitt Rivers' system was accepted, such as at Edinburgh or at the Horniman Museum, his scheme was treated more as a display technique than as a research tool.) To modern social anthropologists, the museum had become outmoded; rejection of the museum approach, in fact, was more or less built into the framework of the field as it was redefined, becoming, in a sense, an anthropological *rite de passage*. And no system more represented that older, object-oriented – as well as 'evolutionary' – viewpoint than that of Pitt Rivers (Plates 8, 9). The 'typological system', at first a system for organizing knowledge and potentially a device for retracing the history of the world, had become for many an embarassing method of display – one that most 'modern' and 'progressive' social anthropologists wanted to disavow. Even before Pitt Rivers' death in 1900, the idea had simply lost its place in the new field.

Acknowledgements

I would like to thank the following institutions and archives for permission to consult, and in some cases quote from, unpublished materials: Bethnal Green Museum (Archives); the British Library (Christy, Lubbock, Way, Perceval Papers; Sotheby Sales Catalogues); The Dorset County Record Office (Pitt Rivers Papers; the Pitt Rivers Museum (Balfour and Tylor Papers); The Salisbury and South Wilts Museum (Pitt Rivers Papers); Leeds City Archives (Lane Fox Papers); University Museum Oxford and the Hopeian Library of Entomology (Westwood Papers); the Society of Antiquaries of London (Archives, Way Papers); the Royal Anthropological Institute (Archives, including the Ethnological Society and Anthropological Society Papers); The Royal Geographical Society (Archives); the Royal United Services Institution (Records); The Public Record Office (Miscellaneous Consular and Military Records and War Office Papers); the Committee for the Ashmolean Museum (Rolleston Papers); the Imperial College of Science (Huxley Papers); and the University of Oxford (Hebdomadal Council Papers and Records of the University Museum). Many other institutions provided facilities for writing and research, most recently the International Centre for the Preservation and Restoration of Cultural Property (ICCROM), Rome, Italy. My thanks especially to the librarians and staff there who provided much needed facilities and help. Also, I would like to thank Dr Nicholas Stanley Price at ICCROM and my wife Betty Ausherman for their comments and suggestions, a number of which have been incorporated into the paper. For advice on the original research, I would like to thank Dennis Britton of the Pitt Rivers Museum, B.A.L. Cranstone, Curator of the Museum and Dr Godfrey Lienhardt of the Institute of Social Anthropology, Oxford, in particular. Special thanks also to Michael and Anthony Pitt Rivers, who provided useful insights on Pitt Rivers and his family background. Finally, I would like to thank the University of Georgia for allowing me time to work on the paper and Yvette Neal for typing an often difficult manuscript.

Notes

1. This paper is based primarily on research carried out for my DPhil thesis, 'Ethnology in the museum: A.H.L.F. Pitt Rivers (1927–1900) and the institutional foundations of British anthropology' (University of Oxford, 1981 unpublished). For more detailed references, and particularly biographical information, the reader should consult that. Other information on Pitt Rivers and his collecting ideas can be found in T.K. Penniman, *A Hundred Years of Anthropology* (London, 1974; first published 1935); Penniman, 'A note on the beginning of anthropology in Oxford' in *Anthropology at Oxford*, Anthropological Society of Oxford, 1953: 11–14; E.B. Tylor, 'Pitt Rivers' in the *Dictionary of National Biography* (1917); H. St G. Gray, 'A memoir of General Pitt Rivers', *Proceedings of the Somerset Archaeological Society* 47 (1900): 123–37; Gray, *Index to 'Excavations in Cranborne Chase'* (Vol. V of the *Excavation* series) (Taunton Castle: privately printed, 1905); Gray, 'Lieutenant-General Pitt Rivers', in *Memoirs of Old Wiltshire* (London, 1906); Gray, 'Recollections on the occasion of the five hundredth meeting of the Oxford University Anthropological Society', *Anthropology at Oxford* (1953): 3–5; B. Blackwood, *The Classification of Artefacts in the Pitt Rivers Museum Oxford* (Pitt Rivers Museum: Oxford, 1970). See also my 'Pitt Rivers and his collection, 1873–1883: the chronicle of a gift horse', *Journal of Anthropological Society of Oxford* 14 (1983), 181–202; and 'Arranging ethnology: A.H.L.F. Pitt Rivers and the typological tradition', in *Objects and Others: Essays on Museums and Material Culture*, George Stocking (ed.) 14–48 (University of Wisconsin Press: Madison, 1985).

2. Augustus Pitt Rivers, 1891. For a more complete bibliography of Pitt Rivers' works consult Chapman, *Ethnology in the Museum*. A published list (although incomplete) is found in Gray, *Index to 'Excavations in Cranborne Chase'*. A number of Pitt Rivers' early papers on material culture are republished in J.L. Meyers, 1906.

3. See particularly his three papers on 'Primitive warfare', 1867b, 1868, 1869b. Henry Wilkinson's *Engines of War* (London, 1841); John Scoffern's *Projectiles and Weapons of War* (London, 1852); C.H. Chesney's *Past and Present State of Firearms* (London, 1852) and Jervis-White Jervise's *The Rifle Musket* (London, 1854) in particular.

4. *Catalogue of the Anthropological Collection Lent by Lane Fox for Exhibition in the Bethnal Green Branch of the South Kensington Museum, June, 1874, Parts I & II*, Science and Art Department of the Committee of Council on Education, (HMSO: London, 1874).

5. Personal Communication, Christine Kelly, Librarian, Royal Geo-

graphical Society. Membership List, *Journal of the Royal Geographical Society* 27 (1857): xiv – xiii.

6. Royal United Services Institution, *Annual Reports*, 1858.
7. Pitt Rivers, 1858: 468. Belcher describes both his work and his collection in *The Last of the Arctic Voyages* (London, 1855). On the Peterick collection: John Petherick, 'On the arms of the Arab and Negro tribes of central Africa', *Journal of the Royal United Services Institution* 4 (1860), 171 – 7.
8. Sotheby's sales catalogues, British Museum.
9. *International Exhibition of 1862: Official Programme* (HMSO: London, 1862).
10. Bertrand Russell and Patricia Russel, 1937. Kate Stanley was to be Bertrand Russell's mother.
11. *Journal of the Kilkenny and Southeast Ireland Archaeological Society*, ns 5 (1884): 3.
12. *Catalogue of the Anthropological Collection* (HMSO: London, 1874): See also Anon., 'General Pitt Rivers', Obituary Notice, *Archaeological Journal* 57 (1900): 174–5.
13. Caulfield's manuscript (1865) reports are in the Pitt Rivers Collection, Salisbury and South Wilts Museum, P2, 4, 6, 7 and 8. His election to the Archaeological Institute is recorded in the Committee Minutes, Archaeological Institute is recorded in the Committee Minutes, Archaeological Institute, 28 January 1864.
14. Certificate of Candidature, Society of Antiquaries of London, 13 October 1863. His election was finalized on 2 June 1864.
15. British Museum, Books of Presents, 1866–8, *f*. 94. See also the *Archaeological Journal* 23 (1866): 149; also Pitt Rivers, 1867c. Pitt Rivers' records of his discovery and transfer are in his collected papers, Salisbury and South Wilts Museum, P2, 4, 6, 7 and 8.
16. Pitt Rivers, 1867c. Bray's principal works were *The Philosophy of Necessity; or the Law or Consequences; as applicable to Mental, Moral and Social Science*, 2 vols (London, 1841; rev. edn. 1865); and *The Education of the Feelings* (London, 1858, rev. edn 1860).
17. *London Illustrated News*, 3 March 1866. His role in the trial is described in the War Office Papers, Public Record Office WO 33/17A: 255–435; WO 81/113: 119–28 and WO 81/114: 11. See also John O'Leary, 1896.
18. Unlabelled Notes, Pitt Rivers Papers, Salisbury and South Wilts Museum, A8c.
19. Their early meeting is documented in William Greenwell, Letter to Albert Way, 7 May 1867, Society of Antiquaries of London, Way Papers.
20. The only published catalogue, which was incomplete, was printed only in 1874. Notes and short lists held in Pitt Rivers Papers at the Salisbury and South Wilts Museum date from a late date, probably the 1880s; the

well-known 'Blue, Black and Red Books' at the Pitt Rivers Museum also appear to date from that period.

21. Pitt Rivers, *Catalogue*, preface. See also Pitt Rivers, 1874, a,b,c. He referred visitors to the Hunterian Collection of the Royal College of Surgeons and, interestingly, to the collection formed by the Anthropological Society of London.

22. See Jomard, 'Caractere et essai de classification d'une collection ethnographique', appendix to *Lettre a M. Fr. de Siebold sur les Collections Ethnographiques* (Publications du Musse d'ethnographie: Paris, 1845). The history of Jomard's idea is discussed at length in E.J. Hamy, 1890 and H.H. Frese, 1960. Jomard's last plea for his idea is found in his paper of 1862.

23. Pitt Rivers, *Catalogue*: 126. Pitt Rivers relied primarily on Siebold's writings on Japanese arms published in his *Archiv zur Beschreibung von Japan*, part 2 (Leyden, 1832–54). Siebold's theories are outlined in Kristian Bahnson, 1888; William, Sturtevant 1969.

24. British Museum, Books of Presents, 1866–8, f. 579; A.W. Franks, *Catalogue of the Christy Collection of Prehistoric Antiquities and Ethnography* (London, 1870): 1.

25. For example, a sale of 24 July 1861; Sotheby's Sales Catalogues, British Museum.

26. Pitt Rivers, *Catalogue*: xiii. Christy's collection at the time of his death, is described most clearly in C.L. Steinhauer, *Catalogue of a Collection of Ancient and Modern Stone Implements and Weapons, Tools and Utensils of the Aborigines of Various Countries in the possession of Henry Christy, F.G.S., etc.* (London, 1862).

27. Membership lists, and Subscribers Ledgers, Ethnological Society of London, and Anthropological Society of London, Royal Anthropological Institute Archives, A25 and A3:1.

28. Royal Anthropological Institute, Council Minutes, Anthropological Society of London, 3 Dec 1867, A3:1.

29. Royal Anthropological Institute, Council Minutes, Ethnological Society of London, 15 June 1868, 23 June 1868, 10 November 1868, A3; Salisbury and South Wilts Museum, Pitt Rivers Papers, P85, P856; British Library, Lubbock Papers, Add MS49643; Pitt Rivers, Letter to Thomas Huxley, 3 September 1868, Imperial College of Science, Huxley Papers.

30. 'Classification Committee', *Journal of the Ethnological Society of London*, ns 1 (1869): 333.

31. 'Report of the Council', *Journal of the Ethnological Society of London*, ns 1 (1869): ix; Royal Anthropological Institute, Council Minutes, Ethnological Society of London, 9 February 1869, A3. The museum was also known as the Museum of Practical Geology. Huxley's position was

that of Chief Lecturer at the closely affiliated School of Mines. In 1862, he was appointed Hunterian Professor at the College of Surgeons, succeeding Owen.

32. Reported in the *Journal of the Ethnological Society of London*, ns 1 (1869): 89–93; 157–77; 218–21.
33. *Catalogue of the Special Exhibition of Ancient Musical Instruments* (London, 1872): 40–6.
34. See, for example, the *London Illustrated News*, 24 October 1865.
35. Pitt Rivers 1874b: 293; Royal Anthropological Institute, Council Minutes, Anthropological Institute, 9 June 1874. A card was printed for the occasion 'to be issued to such visitors as Col. Fox may think fit to indicate'.
36. Science and Art Department, South Kensington Museum, 22nd Annual Report (1864): 443. For the anthropological response: E.B. Tylor, 1875 and G. Busk, 1874.
37. Pitt Rivers, Letter to A.W. Franks, 27 Jun 1880, Pitt Rivers Museum, Balfour Papers.
38. 'Report of the Committee appointed by the Lords of the Committee of Council on Education on the offer made by General Pitt Rivers with regard to his Collection', *Return to an Order of the Honourable The House of Commons*, 27 June 1881.
39. Pitt Rivers, Letter to A.W. Franks, 27 June 1880, Pitt Rivers Museum, Balfour Papers.
40. There are numerous letters from medical advisers among his papers: Salisbury and South Wilts Museum, Pitt Rivers Papers. Pitt Rivers later traced the diagnosis of his illness to 1882: Pitt Rivers, Letter to Herbert Spencer, 2 August 1895, Salisbury and South Wilts Museum, Pitt Rivers Papers, M1–23.
41. Henry Moseley, letter to A.W. Franks, 30 March 1882, Pitt Rivers Museum, Balfour Papers; also, Henry Moseley, Letter to J.W. Westwood, 26 March 1882, University Museum, Hopeian Library of Entomology, Westwood Papers.
42. *Rolleston Memorial Fund* (pamphlet), n.d., University Museum, Hopeian Library of Entomology, Westwood Papers; Salisbury and South Wilts Museum, Pitt Rivers Papers, M38.
43. Oxford University Archives, Hebdomadal Council Papers, 17 April 1882, HD/M/3/4. For further details see Chapman, *Ethnology in the Museum* and 'Pitt Rivers and his collection'.
44. 'Report of Mr. H. Balfour, M.A. Sub-Curator of the Pitt Rivers Museum', *University Gazette*, 2 May 1890.
45. Pitt Rivers, Letter to Henry Balfour, 2 December 1890, Pitt Rivers Museum, Balfour Papers.
46. Pitt Rivers, letter to A.W. Franks, 27 June 1880, Pitt Rivers Museum,

Balfour Papers. On the Farnham Museum, see L.H. Dudley Buxton, 1929.

47. Pitt Rivers, Letter to John Clarell Mansel-Playdel, 11 Oct 1885, Salisbury and South Wilts Museum, Pitt Rivers Papers, M36b; Pitt Rivers, 'Address Bath 1888': 829.

48. 'Handley, Primrose League Gathering', *Dorset County Chronicle*, 17 May 1888 (ostensibly a verbatim account). A different draft version of the speech is found in the Salisbury and South Wilts Museum, Pitt Rivers Papers, M31.

49. See Thompson, *Catalogue of the Pitt Rivers Papers in the Salisbury and South Wilts Museum*, TS, 1979: 71.

50. Pitt Rivers, Letter to F.W. Rudler, 23 May 1898, Salisbury and South Wilts Museum, Pitt Rivers Papers, Correspondence.

Bibliography

Bahnson, K., 'Ethnographical museums', *Archaeological Review* 2, 1888: 1–16.

Balfour, H., 'On the structure and affinities of the composite bow', *Journal of the Anthropological Institute* 18, 1889: 220–46.

Burrow, J.W., 'Evolution and anthropology in 1860's: the Anthropological Society of London, 1863–71', *Victorian Studies* 7, 1963: 137–54.

Burrow, J.W., *Evolution and Society: A Study in Victorian Social Theory* (Cambridge University Press: Cambridge, 1966).

Busk, G., 'Presidential address', *Journal of the Anthropological Institute* 4, 1874: 469–500.

Buxton, L.H.D., *The Pitt Rivers Museum, Farnham, Farnham Dorset*, The Farnham Museum, 1929.

Caulfield, R., 'Remains of the Aboriginal inhabitants of Ireland' *Gentleman's Magazine*, ns 18, part 1, 1865: 707–10.

Crawfurd, J., 'On Sir Charles Lyell's *Antiquity of Man* and on Prof. Huxley's *Evidence as to Man's Place in Nature*', *Transactions Ethnological Society of London* 3, 1862: 58–70.

Crawfurd, J., 'On the early migrations of man', *Transactions of the Ethnological Society of London* 3, 1864: 335–50.

Forbes, E., 'Museums as instruments of education', *The Art Journal* 5, 1853: 282–5.

Forbes, E., 'On the educational uses of museums', *American Journal of Science* 1854: 340–52.

Frese, H.H., *Anthropology of the Public* (Leiden, 1960).

Gray, E., 'Presidential address to section D of the *British Association's Report of the British Association for the Advancement of Science*', 1864: 76–86.

174 *Museum economics and the community*

Grayson, D.K., *The Establishment of Human Antiquity* (University of Washington Press: Seattle, 1983).

Greenwood, T., *Museums and Art Galleries* (London, 1888).

Haddon, A.C., 'Pitt Rivers: obituary notice' *Nature* 42, 1900: 59–60.

Hamy, E.J., *Les Origines du Musee d'ethnographie, histoire et documents.* (Publications du Musee d'Ethnographie: Paris, 1890).

Hunt, J., 'Introductory address on the study of anthropology', *Anthropological Review* 1, 1863a: 1–20.

Hunt, J., 'Notes on the antiquity of man', *Anthropological Review* 1863b: 72–107.

Huxley, T., 'Methods and results of ethnology' *Fortnightly Review* 1, 1865: 257–77.

Huxley, T., 'The advisableness of imparting natural knowledge', *Fortnightly Review* 3, 1866: 626–52.

Huxley, T., 'On the distribution of the races of mankind and its bearing on the antiquity of man', *Trans of the 3rd Session of the International Congress of Prehistoric Archaeology* 1869: 92–6.

Huxley, T., 'On the geographical distribution of the chief modifications of man', *Journal of the Ethnological Society of London*, ns 2, 1870: 404–12.

Jomard, E.-F., 'Quelques mots sur l'ethnographie Asiatique', *Review Orientale Americaine* 8, 1862: 75–7.

Knox, R., *The Races of Men: A Fragment* (London, 1862a).

Knox, R., *The Races of Man: A Philosophical Inquiry into the Influence of Race over the Destinies of Nature* (London, 1862b).

Lienhardt, R.-G., *Social Anthropology* (Oxford University Press: Oxford, 1964).

Meyers, J.-L., (ed.), *The Evolution of Culture and Other Essays* (Clarendon Press: Oxford, 1906).

O'Leary, J., *Recollections of Fenians and Fenianism*, 2 vols (London, 1896).

Perry P.J., *British Agriculture 1875–1914* (London, 1973).

Pitt Rivers, A., *The Instruction of Musketry* (Hythe School of Musketry: Hythe, 1854).

Pitt Rivers, A., 'The improvement of the rifle as a weapon for general use', *Journal of the Royal United Services Institution* 2, 1858: 453–88.

Pitt Rivers, A., 'On an ivory peg-top shaped object from Ireland', *Proceedings Society of Antiquaries of London*, second series 3, 1865: 395–6.

Pitt Rivers, A., 'Objects of the Roman Period found at great depth in the vicinity of the Old London Wall' *Archaeological Journal* 24, 1866a: 61–4.

Pitt Rivers, A., 'Roovesmore Fort and Stones Inscribed with Oghams in the Parish Aglish, County Cork' *Archaeological Journal* 23, 1866b: 149 and 24, 1867c: 129–39.

Pitt Rivers, A., 'A Description of certain piles near London Wall and Southwark, possible the remains of Pile Buildings', *Journal of Anthropological Society of London* 5, 1867a: lxxi–lxxxii.

Pitt Rivers, A., 'Primitive warfare', *Journal of the Royal United Services Institution* 11, 1867b: 612–43; 12, 1868: 399–439; 13, 1869b; 509–59.

Pitt Rivers, A., 'Memoir on the hill forts of Sussex', *Proceedings of the Society of Antiquaries of London*, second series, 4, 1868: 70–80.

Pitt Rivers, A., 'On the discovery of flint implements of Palaeolithic type in the gravel of the Thames Valley at Acton and Ealing', *Report of the British Association for the Advancement of Science*, 1869a: 130–2.

Pitt Rivers, A., 'Address to the Department of Anthropology of the British Association of Knighton', *Report of the British Association for the Advancement of Science*, 1872a: 157–74.

Pitt Rivers, A., 'Questions for explorers (with special reference to Arctic Explorations)', *Journal of the Anthropological Institute* 2, 1872b: 296–306.

Pitt Rivers, A., 'Enquiries relating to drawing, carving and ornamentations', *Journal of the Anthropological Institute* 2, 1872c: 301–2.

Pitt Rivers, A., 'On Early Modes of Navigation', *Journal of the Anthropological Institute* 4, 1874a: 399–435.

Pitt Rivers, A., 'On the principles of classification adopted in the arrangement of his anthropological collection, now exhibited in the Bethnal Green Museum', *Journal of the Anthropological Institute* 4, 1874b: 293–308.

Pitt Rivers, A., 'Note on the chest measurements of recruits', *Journal of the Anthropological Institute* 5, 1874c: 101–6.

Pitt Rivers, A., 'On the evolution of culture', *Journal of the Anthropological Institute* 7, 1875a: 375–89.

Pitt Rivers, A., 'Excavations in Cissbury Camp, Sussex', *Journal of the Anthropological Institute* 5, 1875b: 375–89.

Pitt Rivers, A., 'Report on Measurements of the whole of the officers and men of Second Royal Survey Militia', *Journal of the Anthropological Institute* 6, 1877: 443–57.

Pitt Rivers, A., 'Excavations at Mount Caburn Camp near Lewes, conducted in 1877 and 1878', *Archaeologia* 57, 1880: 423–95.

Pitt Rivers, A., *Excavations in Cranborne Chase, near Rushmore, on the Borders of Dorset and Wilts.* (Rushmore: Printed Privately, 1882a).

Pitt Rivers, A., 'On excavations in the earthwork called Dane's Dyke, at Flamborough in October 1879, and on the earthworks of the Yorkshire Wolds', *Journal of Anthropological Institute* 11, 1882b: 460–83.

Pitt Rivers, A., *An Address Delivered at the Opening of the Dorset Museum on Tuesday, January 7th 1884* (Dorchester, 1884).

Pitt Rivers, A., 'Address as President of the Anthropological Section of the British Association, Bath, Sept. 6th 1888', *Report of the British Association for the Advancement of Science* 1888: 825–35.

Pitt Rivers., A. 'Typological museums, as exemplified by the Pitt Rivers Museum at Oxford, and his provincial museum at Farnham, Dorset', *Journal of the Society of Arts* 40, 1891: 115–22.

Pitt Rivers, A., *Antique Works of Art from Benin* (Rushmore: printed privately, 1900).

Richter, D.C., *Riotous Victorians* (University of Ohio Press: Ohio, 1981).

Russell, B., and Russell, P., *The Amberley Papers: The Letters and Diaries of Bertrand Russell's Parents*, vol. II (W.W. Norton: New York, 1937).

Stocking, G., 'What's in a name: the origins of the Royal Anthropological Institute (1837–1871)', *Man*, ns 6, 1971: 369–90.

Sturtevant, W., 'Does anthropology need museums?', *Proceedings of the Biological Society of Washington* 82, 1969: 619–49.

Thompson, M.W., *General Pitt Rivers: Evolution and Archaeology in the Nineteenth Century* (Moonraker Press: Bradford-on-Avon, 1977).

Tylor, E.B., 'Revnue of the catalogue of the anthropological collection of Col. Lane Fox', *The Academy* 6, 1875: 460.

Tylor, E.B., 'Pitt Rivers', *Dictionary of National Biography, First Supplement*, vol III (1917): 268–70.

Urry, J., 'Notes and queries on anthropology and the development of field methods in British anthropology, 1870-1920', *Proceedings of the Royal Anthropological Institute*, 1972: 45–57.

van Keuren, D., 'Museums and ideology: Augustus Pitt Rivers, anthropological museums and social change in later Victorian Britain', *Victorian Studies* 28, 1984: 171–89.

Wilde, W., *A Descriptive Catalogue of the Museum of Antiquities of the Royal Irish Academy, Parts I–III* (Royal Irish Academy: Dublin, 1857–62).

7

The Elepe's beadwork:
a question of legitimacy

CHARLES HUNT

Introduction

At a meeting of the Central Native Council in Lagos on 25 February 1903 a Yoruba chief was chastised by the Governor, Sir William MacGregor for transgressing custom and offending traditional values by assuming a beaded crown to which he was not entitled. The proceedings of the Council and the language used illuminate the subversion of Yoruba ritual values and their appropriation by a liberal-minded governor for colonial, capitalist ends. The confiscated beaded regalia now belong to the British Museum and are on display in Aberdeen. Here, they continue to play out the humiliation of the Elepe and the manipulation of Yoruba beliefs in the interests of European pragmatism. On the same day, in southern Ethiopia, a meeting between a British official and an Abyssinian chief has been recorded which invites comparison both because of the attraction of coincidence and because it too raised the issue of the relation between words and things. It is this issue, one of particular importance to museums, which this paper sets out to discuss.

The Elepe's beadwork

Aberdeenshire has a long and honorable association with Africa: honorable in the sense that as a community it was active and influential in the abolition of the slave trade and because it sent more missionaries and doctors to Africa than merchants and soldiers (Hargreaves, 1981). Inevitably, the university received African ethnography from about 1800 onwards and this was brought together with other cultural materials in 1907 to form the Anthropological Museum in Marischal College. One of the most important contributors was Sir William MacGregor, born the son of a farm servant in Donside, Aberdeenshire, who rose to be a distinguished colonial administrator (Joyce, 1971).

MacGregor took up his appointment as Governor of Lagos in May, 1899. One of his earliest acts was to establish the Central Native Council. He carried through his ordinance against the opposition of the Aborigines Protection Society, African members of the Legislative Council and with only the half-hearted support of the Colonial Office. His avowed intention was to reassert the power of the traditional Yoruba chiefs which was being undermined by decisions of junior European officials and challenged from within their own states by educated Africans: 'All these causes have eclipsed the authority of the hereditary chiefs, and that too at a time when their active intervention as rulers is more required and needed than it ever was before.[1] The Lagos Press, on the contrary, saw his legislation as 'nothing less than a subversion of existing law and custom... the destruction of native organisations and the substitution of hybrid organisations of the various provinces of which the Central Native Council in Lagos, with the Governor as President, will be the ruling spirit and final arbiter'.[2]

These contradictory elements – assertion of the chiefs' authority but defined within colonial laws – resulted from MacGregor's application of the principle of indirect rule. It has been claimed that: 'during... his Governorship the justification of indirect administration as a method of colonial rule reached a level of consistency and rationalisation never before attained' (Aberibigbe, 1953: 343).

MacGregor's early colonial career was spent in Fiji in the entourage of the colony's first British Governor, Sir Arthur Gordon. The history of that administration and Gordon's determination to rule through the Fijian chiefly hierarchy has been summarized by Peter France (France, 1969). One result of the policy was to consolidate the social order – part real, part product of European misunderstanding – in perpetuity; a process referred to by France as the 'founding of an Orthodoxy'. In Fiji the Orthodoxy prevails and the chiefly system is a powerful conservative factor in issues of political and economic development. MacGregor went on to apply his version of indirect rule in New Guinea and Lagos. It involved the identification of a traditional ruling elite and the confirmation of that élite in its powers and privileges with the colonial power at the apex of the hierarchy. A meeting held in Government House, Lagos, on the evening of 25 February 1903, is an illustration of the policy at work.

On that day the Central Native Council was convened in order to settle a dispute between two Ijebu (Remo) chiefs, the Akarigbo of Sagamu and the Elepe of Epe, over the right of the Elepe to wear a crown with a beaded fringe – a prerogative of members of the House of Odudua. The Governor chaired the proceedings and he allowed each chief to bring ten witnesses elderly men who would be able to inform the Council as to what had hitherto been the custom about the wearing of a crown by an Elepe. If these numbers and the Governor's sense of fair play are reminiscent of a cricket match the analogy is carried forward by the introduction of a second umpire in the person of the Oni of Ife. MacGregor was at pains to assure the assembly that the Oni attended out of friendship for the Governor and not because he had been ordered to do so. The Oni's unswerving politeness makes it unclear whether this was actually the case. In any event, his presence in itself marked a breach with tradition since no previous Oni had been known to leave his palace after his accession except for religious or state ceremonies within the capital and his journey caused consternation within the land.

MacGregor sought to reconcile the transgression by means of a somewhat tortured and Eurocentric rationalisation. to quote from the *Lagos Gazette*:

> The Governor... hoped the Oni would keep a quiet mind as regards the ancient tradition of Ife. His Excellency believed that there was nothing in the national tradition to forbid the Oni travelling in the Governor's special hammock and riding to Lagos in the train. If the tradition of Ife forbade the Oni travelling in a hammock, His Excellency felt sure that the reference must have been to an ordinary hammock. His Excellency could not conceive that travelling in the train was forbidden by the tradition of Ife.[3]

The Oni expressed concern about meeting the Akarigbo and the Elepe face to face, another contravention of tradition. MacGregor's solution was to have the chief seated with his back to the assembly. Here we have no imperial Governor riding roughshod over native tradition but one, rather, who is so mindful of its importance that he creates and invents, stretches and bends it to his use. At the same time as he distorts a tradition he confirms it. This is reminiscent of MacGregor's mentor, Sir Arthur Gordon, who presided over the installation of a Fijian High Chief in 1880. Gordon recorded in his journal: 'At the conclusion of the ceremonies, I declared the bowl of yaqona just taken from the tanoa to be that for the drinking of the "na turaga ko na Roko Ratu Tui Cakaudrove" thereby confirming that designation of Ratu Lala who drank its contents' (France, 1969: 25). The string of chiefly epithets is, as Peter France points out, without meaning in Fijian custom, and the ceremonial action which Gordon appeared to think of such significance can have made no difference to the relationship between Ratu Lala and his people. We might consider that MacGregor, by inviting the Oni of Ife to arbitrate publically in this dispute and investing his judgement with the authority of the colonial power was attributing to this traditional ruler an explicit and active role in Yoruba political affairs which his ritual primacy had not previously accorded him.

The meeting opened with an address by the Governor. The two important points to be considered by the Council were to safeguard the body of Chiefs by preventing a man who was not entitled to wearing a crown from doing so, and to preserve the right of an individual to wearing a crown if he was entitled to do so.

In answer to a question from the Governor, the Oni said that he had never before heard of an Elepe assuming the right to wear a crown. The Oni also explained that on occasion of original assignment of a crown a fee of £50 at least was paid to the Oni of Ife. This fee was demanded only from the first ruler of the territory for which the crown is assigned. But there was no evidence in Ife that an Elepe had at any time paid this fee.

The Governor now observed that as neither the Elepe nor his fathers before him had paid anything to the Oni of Ife for a crown the Elepe could not, according to native *law and usage*, wear a crown (author's emphasis).

The Governor asked the Oni whether the Elepe could be permitted to wear a crown if he now paid £50. The Oni replied that all crowns were hereditary and that a man could not wear a crown if his fathers before him had not put on a crown. The power vested in the Oni of Ife was to confirm the right to the title. All crowns were hereditary.

The Governor now asked the Elepe what he had to say in exculpation of his act. The Elepe stated that he obtained the crown he was wearing from his people and that the council of the town told him that it was from Ife. They also told him that both the Elepe and the Akarigbo used to wear crowns.

Ignoring the contradiction in the Oni's statement and having judged the case against the Elepe proved on the basis of that statement the Governor invited opinions from members of the

Council some of which illustrate the confusion occurring when legal specificity meets ritual ambiguity.

> Kasuma Giwa:– We thank the Governor for the trouble he is taking over this matter. We pray for the prosperity of the British Government. We also thank our father the Oni of Ife for having come to enlighten us on this matter. We never before heared of the Oni leaving his town. We never heared of an Oni leaving Ife, the cradle of our race. I have listened with great attention to what the Oni said. But I should like to ascertain from the Elepe who were the Council that presented him with a crown.

The senior member of the Elepe's Council was called in and questioned. He stated: 'We made the present Elepe the Elepe of Epe, and presented him with a crown which his father had brought from Ife'. The Governor hereupon informed the Elepe's councillor that the Oni had satisfied the Council that no former Elepe had a crown or paid the fee due for wearing a crown. There was no doubt that the present man was an Elepe, but there was at the same time no doubt that he was not entitled to wear a crown. There was no evidence that his predecessors before him wore a crown.

The Bale of Ebute Metta (Egba):	I stand by what the Oni says and what the Governor decides.
Chief Ojura:	It is a wonderful thing to see the Oni at Lagos. I believe the Oni of Ife and the Akarigbo are right in this matter. It is an old question. Many years ago the dispute led to war. But it is now being settled quietly with the authority of the Oni.
Chief Obanikoro:	The Oni is the only authority on this subject and we abide by his decision. The crown question is a most important question. It affects not only one man but also the whole town. And it often ends in war.

The Elepe was fined one hundred pounds and his beadwork was confiscated. The Oni of Ife received a stipend of one hundred pounds a year and the Governor undertook to intervene in his dispute with Ibadan. On leaving the Oni requested the Governor, as a special favour, to place his crown on his head. The Governor did so and told him that His Excellency considered crowns of great importance and that their sacred character should always be preserved. In his testimony the Oni had listed twenty one obas entitled to wear beaded crowns: this compares with the forty-one claimants to Ife crowns recorded by Ojo in 1966 (Ojo, 1966).

Beadwork and language

There are two aspects of the meeting that deserve comment: the language and the beadwork. MacGregor's language or, to be more exact, the summaries and verbatim extracts recorded in the *Lagos Gazette* seem a choice example of colonial appropriation of African beliefs and customs to achieve colonial/capitalist ends. We do not have to understand MacGregor as a stereotypical imperialist to know that his aims were continued British administration of Lagos and more effective exploitation of the colony and its hinterland through improved agriculture and medical care. The successful achievement of his aims required the assertion of western rational, experimentally verifiable standards over African sacred, ritually validated ones. The castigation of the Elepe of Epe was made an opportunity to board and capture African customs by inserting those symbols of European power, the steam train and the Government's hammock and to master the political situation by converting the Oni of Ife's ambiguous ritual and symbolic status into quasi-legal authority.

A paper by William Pietz, in a volume of post-structuralist essays, contains an analysis of a passage from H.M. Stanley's *The Congo and the Founding of its Free State* describing a river journey past a magically potent (in African thought) and dangerous rock. Pietz distinguishes an African tribal from a western capitalist mode of linguistic apprehension and illustrates how Stanley's written discourse acts to subvert and colonise the African view by intervening in his informants narrative and revaluing the superstitious interpretation to serve an enlightened end. Pietz writes:

> the ideological allegory of this anecdote concerns the way the scientifically enlightened capitalist mind . . . gains ironic mastery over figurative language and hence not only frees itself from superstition but can free the unenlightened from superstition by revaluing their narratives. Capitalist desire is essentially the desire for the liberation, control and direction of flows of all sorts; it is the subversion of all concrete cultural and territorial codes (Pietz, 1987: 274).

The cultural and territorial codes at issue in our Lagos meeting may be understood as the status of the Oni and the prohibitions governing his travelling outside his own palace. They are mastered by the revaluation of customary belief through the insertion of the Governor's hammock representing European political dominance and the railway representing European technological superiority and commercial desire. The meeting can be seen as a metaphor for the pacification of the Yoruba by the appropriation of their belief system.

If the Council meeting was a metaphor perhaps it can also be interpreted as ritual. Monica Wilson writes:

> Rituals reveal values at their deepest level . . . men express in ritual what moves them most and since the form of expression is conventionalised and obligatory it is the values of the group that are revealed. I see in the study of rituals the key to an understanding of the essential constitution of human societies (Wilson, 1954: 241).

By these criteria the interaction in Government House on the day in question falls short of ritual, being in the nature of an ad hoc rather than a prescribed occasion, governed by arbitrary rather than obligatory procedures and with participants subscribing in only the loosest fashion to a common set of values. Yet within a structured framework combining western legal formality and African social conformity it included symbolic elements expressing the subordination of custom to technology and of implicit to explicit understanding. Perhaps ritual also has the quality of continual reaffirmation while legal process has the quality of finality. The first is biodegradable. The other can be superceded but not deleted. The record of the Elepe's disgrace remains with us, as does his beaded regalia.

Most of the anthropological material collected by Sir William MacGregor was given to the Aberdeen University Museum or to several Australian museums. The beadwork, exceptionally, was passed to the British Museum presumably because it was officially removed from the Elepe and remained official by being placed in the national repository. It was evidence and remains evidence of the Elepe's hubris. In 1984 the British Museum generously allowed Aberdeen University to borrow the beaded crown, cap and boots for a new anthropological display where they are presently on display as still evidence of the misdemeanor. The public humiliation of the Elepe continues to be played out, silently and innocuously, in the north-east corner of Scotland. What other meaning can the museum place on these objects. They are patently not symbols of divine kingship: to quote from views expressed during the Council meeting, 'if the crown does not come from Ife it is a worthless thing'. 'The Elepe's crown is a crown of shame.' They might more accurately be described as symbols of the Elepe's non-status if such a thing is possible. The museum label reads:

Beaded regalia confiscated from the Elepe of Epe by Sir William
MacGregor, Governor of Lagos, in 1903. The Elepe had assumed the
regalia, including the crown, although he had no hereditary right to do so.
He was rebuked for this act by a Council or Chiefs under the authority of
the Oni of Ife, a sacred King.

This may be seen as rehearsing indefinitely the colonial drama which
occurred in Government House on that evening.

Museums are by-products of the capitalist impulse which drove
Europeans to colonise the distant and the past. The very endurance of
objects upon which museums pride themselves transfixes the meaning of things, the networks of dialectic which would otherwise have
been dissolved or re-arranged in the current of cultural fictions. Their
collections are appropriations of other peoples beliefs and actions –
imposing sense where there was non-sense and order where there was
no order. It is an exceptional opportunity to be able to show objects
as participants in acrimonious debate. Too often museums represent
artefacts as elements in contingent structures of relations rather than
as affective agents in ideological dispute where meaning is fluid and
responsive to historical circumstance.

The Ethiopian case

On the same day and at approximately the same hour that the Central
Native Council was meeting in Lagos another, less formal meeting
was taking place in a camp somewhere between Addis Ababa and
Lake Rudolph. This was between Mr John Baird, a British political
officer, and Bash Dugge, an Abyssinian chiefly official. Coinciden-
tally Baird, too, was from Donside in Aberdeenshire and he would
also donate ethnographical material to Aberdeen university.[4] To
complete the coincidence, both MacGregor and Baird were responsible for journeys to Aberdeenshire by high-ranking Africans:
Baird invited Ras Makonnen, Governor of Harar province, in 1902,
and MacGregor hosted a visit by the Alake of Abeokuta to Aberdeen
in 1904.

John Baird, later Lord Stonehaven of Urie, accompanied an
expedition to define a border between the expanding Ethiopian
empire of Menelik II and British East Africa. Some of the implications of this expedition have been discussed elsewhere (Hunt, 1988).
The expedition had an Abyssinian escort with whom Baird developed

an increasingly strained relationship. He was frequently engaged in recriminations with their leaders, so that it is perhaps not quite so unexpected that his confrontation with an Abyssinian chief should coincide with MacGregor's chastisement of a Yoruba chief.

The interview has some resemblances to the Yoruba Council meeting. Baird's Western capitalist determination to achieve the temporal and territorially defined objectives of mapping a border within a limited period of time confront an Abyssinian priority emphasising courtesy and acknowledgement of rank; the instrumental versus the metaphorical. The role played in Lagos by the beaded crown, tangible symbol of chiefship, around which swirl the rights and obligations, beliefs, antagonisms and the language of the actors is mirrored in Baird's tent by two sheep. They are not the issue at stake but they are the locus of the action. To quote from Baird's diary:

> I therefore saw him and asked him what he meant by sending me such a message as he had sent in the morning. He replied that yesterday I had kicked him out of my tent like a dog: but that as I had sent for him he had come to ask me not to be angry with him and to offer me a couple of sheep – I told him that I could not accept any present unless I had an explanation of this morning's conduct. He made some rather lame excuses, etc., etc. He said that everything we had wanted he had always brought – beef, sheep, camels etc. and he did not think he had fallen short of his duty in any way. I told him that we had not come here for the pleasure of eating Boran sheep and cattle or to be done in the eye over Boran camels, but to do a bit of work which we had undertaken on the Emperor's behalf and that every obstacle had been put in the way of our completing our task. I consented to take his sheep telling him I had no desire to quarrel with him, but he must remember . . . that we were liable to return presents if we were displeased.

Mr Baird might as well have been at Harrods. Whether or not the return of 'presents' had any institutionalised meaning for Africans in the Horn, it is clear that Baird considered the action to be a resounding expression of contempt and he offers an example of a European colonial giving contractual significance to a symbolic gesture. The sheep were not included among the African objects which Baird presented to the Anthropological Museum. If they had been they would probably have suffered the same fate as the beadwork – i.e. being represented as 'fixed evidence' when they were, in fact, a spontaneous, momentary gesture.

Some implications

The Elepe's crown and the Bashe's sheep illustrate the status of objects as ingredients in individualistic confrontations, as catalysts in disputes which were ideological, verbal and gesticulatory. Their symbolic value is not inherent but ascribed by the actors in particular dramas at particular moments. The preservation of African objects in European museums does not represent a fixing of their defined or yet-to-be defined significance but is, on the contrary, a prolongation of the dialectic which they were created to generate. They will be polemical for as long as they exist. Mary Douglas has written: 'At this time, anthropologists, beset by philosophical quandaries from which they see no escape are content to treat the best undertaking they can report as well-observed, deeply interpreted fictional texts' (Douglas, 1980: 124). Museum anthropology must attempt to be at least as tentative and self-critical when it seeks to mediate between African objects and Western objectivity.

Notes

1. MacGregor to Colonial Office, 11 November 1901, 147/157/45594.
2. Editorial, *Lagos Standard*, 25 September 1901.
3. Minutes of Central Native Council 24 February 1903, *Lagos Government Gazette*, 28 February 1903, CO 150/11, 165–70.
4. J.L. Baird, typescript journal, Aberdeen University Library, MS3064, vols 134, 137–40, 142, 145, 30 October 1902–21 March 1903.

Bibliography

Aberibigbe, A.A.B., 'Expansion of the Lagos protectorate 1863–1900', PhD thesis (London University, 1959).
Douglas, M., *Evans-Prichard* (Brighton, 1980).
France, P., *The Charter of the Land: Custom and Colonisation in Fiji* (Oxford University Press: Melbourne, 1969).
Hargreaves, J., *Aberdeenshire to Africa: Northeast Scots and the British Overseas Expansion* (Aberdeen University Press: Aberdeen, 1981).
Hunt, C.G., 'Animals as metaphor: the Butter Expedition 1902/3' in *The Exploitation of Animals in Africa*, J.C. Stone (ed.) (Aberdeen University Press: Aberdeen, 1988).

Joyce, R.B., *Sir William MacGregor* (Oxford University Press: Melbourne, 1971).

Ojo, G.J.A., *Yoruba Culture: A Geographical Analysis* (London, 1966).

Pietz, W., 'The phonograph in Africa: international phonocentricism from Stanley to Sarnoff' in *Poststructuralism and the Question of History*, D. Attridge, G. Bennington and R. Young (eds) (Cambridge, 1987): 263–85.

Wilson, M., 'Nyakyusa ritual and symbolism', *American Anthropologist* 56 (2) 1954: 228–41.

PART THREE
Reviews edited by
Eilean Hooper-Greenhill

The video *Building New Audiences for Museums*

National Museum, New Delhi, India

The Scottish Museums Council is one of the most active organizations in the United Kingdom. In 1986, it launched a three-year project, 'The Leisure Learning Programme' with the aim of 'encouraging more people of all ages and from all walks of life to visit museums by providing a wide range of activities and events.' Throughout the three years of the programme a wide variety of activities such as touring exhibitions, handling sessions, illustrated talks, workshops, dance and music, were conducted in more than twenty museums and galleries around Scotland for different target audiences. The programme was organized in collaboration with other organizations including the Scottish Council for Disability, libraries, community education departments, film theatres, and children's play schemes.

After the completion of the project a video was brought out which demonstrates how leisure learning can change a museum from a static, dead and quiet place to a lively cultural centre. The video and the accompanying booklet show the concern for the museums in developing new audiences, and speak of the success of the Scottish Museums Council in building new audiences by providing a variety of opportunities for participation in a range of activities. The video and the booklet present four case studies to stimulate interest in the approach used by the Scottish museums that combines learning with leisure. Each case study offers a sample of the ingeniously planned and indefatigably carried out programmes that demonstrate how many more people of all kinds can be brought into museums. Obviously the flops, if any, have not been included.

The video is produced using slides and is pleasant to look at because of the smooth flow created by dissolving one slide into the next. At the same time the video has become monotonous due to the use of too many slides. In this twenty-minute video over two hundred slides have been used. The video could have been made more interesting by reducing the number of slides and introducing

191

movements by zooming in or zooming out, or sideways movements. The visual quality of some of the slides is also not good. Perhaps the preparation of the video was an afterthought and therefore choice of slides was limited.

There is no doubt that this video is an important document. It is intended as a starting-point and example for other museums, art galleries, historic houses, libraries, or other types of cultural organizations. The case studies exhibit a range of educational possibilities presented by the museums that can serve as models for other organizations wishing to conduct similar activities to reach out for new audiences. It can be very useful for museum personnel, particularly museum educators in developing countries where there are no such programmes in most of the museums.

Building New Audiences for Museums was produced by the Scottish Museums Council, 1989.

Children's Clothes by Clare Rose

PAM INDER

Department of Art History, Stoke-on-Trent Polytechnic

Surprisingly little has been written about the history of children's clothes, and so this book is especially welcome. *Children's Clothes* covers the history of children's costume from 1750 to 1985. The layout is straightforward. There is a brief introduction, followed by three parts covering the periods 1750–1820, 1820–1890 and 1890–1895. Each part contains three chapters entitled 'Babies', 'Girls' and 'Boys'. There is a short glossary, a select bibliography and a series of footnotes directing the reader to sources of further information. The author has drawn on a wide range of sources – portraits, photographs, autobiographies, treaties on childcare, advertisements, catalogues, and dressmaking and knitting patterns. She has also studied numerous specimens of costume in museum collections. The book is easy to read, and a careful scholarly piece of work. Despite the shortage of information, the author has made a brave attempt to deal with the dress of working-class children as well as those of the middle and upper classes.

However, given the amount of material Clare Rose has collected, and the amount of material she has obviously had to leave out, it seems a pity that this could not have been a longer book – or even several books. The references and quotations are often tantalizingly brief. I would, for example, have liked much more information about Locke's and Rousseau's writings and more quotations from Dr Cadogan. For the later nineteenth and twentieth centuries there is a wealth of material available from autobiographies, magazines, photographs, advertising literature and catalogues which this book can only hint at. Even sources which are quoted, like Gwen Raverat's *Period Piece* and Molly Hughes's *A London Family 1870–1900* contain much more information than is used. Much twentieth-century material has been omitted altogether. What of Ladybird, Start-rite, Mothercare or Laura Ashley?

The book contains 8 colour illustrations and 128 black and white ones, and of these over 90 are of costumes in museum collections. Overall, the standard of the illustrations is fairly high – but they do show just how appalling the majority of museum dummies are: it is difficult to decide which come out the worst – the headless, limbless torsos on wood or metal stands, the figures with heads but stylized features (these look particularly blank and menacing in photographs) or the 'natural' figures with staring eyes, too much hair and strange postures! Still on the subject of illustrations, it seems a pity that so many (7) are reproduced from Manchester City Museum's 'Picture Book Number Seven" of 1959, which shows garments worn by child models. While this was acceptable practice in 1959, and charming as the illustrations undoubtedly are, it seems wrong to reuse them at a time when curatorial opinion, quite rightly, is so much against the use of live models. In many ways, more contemporary illustrations of garments in the form of photographs, fashion plates, portraits and illustrations might have been of more use than so many illustrations of 'curator interpretations' of how children wore clothes.

But these are quibbles. Given the length of the book – which presumably was dictated by the publishers – this is the most useful reference book in print for the collector or curator of costume, dealing as it does with the period within which most of our collections fall. There may well be a place for more detailed publications about children's costume. I hope Clare Rose is going to write some of them.

Children's Clothes by Clare Rose published by Batsford £25 hbk ISBN 0 7134 57414 and £14.95 pbk ISBN 0 7134 64445, 1989.

Picture Power: Visual Depiction and Social Relations, Gordon Fyfe and John Law (eds)

SUSAN PEARCE

Department of Museum Studies, University of Leicester

The volume, the 35th in its series, gathers together ten substantial essays, divided into three sections labelled 'Visualization and social reproduction', 'On the social production of visual difference' and 'On visualization as *power*': the choice of language gives a fair idea of what most of the writing in the papers will be like, and generally it meets expectations although some contributions are much better than others. Two of the papers, by Bud and Bann, deal directly with museums, which is another way of saying that these two papers use the word 'museum' in their titles, but many of the other essays, dealing as they do with the potential aspect of paintings and viewed images of all kinds, discuss matters of the greatest relevance to museums, especially museum exhibition.

The first section includes papers by Bruno Latour, Stephen Bann, Gordon Fyfe and Belinda Loftus. Latour sets out to show that the turn of the fifteenth and sixteenth centuries saw a shift between two regimes of religious painting, in which the depiction of an 'eternal' event became instead the representation of a historical sequence: 'the event of the Passion is not represented anew as if it were happening again and was contemporaneous with the Ambassadors (in Holbein's picture of the same name); it is replaced by a crucifix that alludes to a past and closed event which is not depicted'. This is an interesting cluster of ideas, which is beginning to attract a good deal of attention. Among other things, it has a bearing on the way in which collections were made and viewed during the same period.

Bann, in a paper entitled 'Views of the Past – reflections on the treatment of historical objects and museums of history (1750–1850)', argues that 'viewing the past' has a specific significance when it is seen in terms of the modes of interpretation which came naturally to antiquarians and collectors between 1750 and 1850, who were concerned to revalue and represent the past in a revelatory way. They gave a strong affective character to the process of historical and archaeological retrieval because they shared a passionate relationship of desire towards the decaying objects which they salvaged, to which they assigned a particular value that derived chiefly from an appreciation that the objects were 'historical', that they were 'old', and were to be identified with the visible signs of age and decay. This, in turn, led to the creation of dramatic narratives of the hitherto neglected past. Bann relates these ideas about 'age-value' to several important early collections, including that made by Brian Fausset, and to several early museums opened as exhibitions, including Sir John Soane's Museum, Alexandre Lenoir's Musée des Monuments Français at the Convent of the Petits-Augustin in Paris, and Alexandre du Sommerard's Musée de Cluny also in Paris. Bann's paper contains rather a wide spread of ideas, but they are imaginative ideas capable of shedding light on some very obscure passages in the development of the historical sense, and more work published by this writer on the nineteenth-century museums would be very welcome.

The second section begins with a paper by Bud, 'The Myth and the Machine: seeing Science through Museum Eyes'. Bud writes as a curator who was closely involved with the creation of the major new Chemical Industry Gallery at the Science Museum, London. The museum is seen to have acted as a broker in bringing together diverse interests, and the paper describes the negotiations involved in selecting objects, text and physical environment, and the translation of goals during the process. Bud suggests that an exhibition is a combination of mythic form and machine and concludes that the qualities of the machine get the upper hand as the array of practical problems arising from exhibition realization have to be solved. Between the idea and the exhibit falls the shadow, as Eliot might have put it; Bud's description has the unmistakable ring of familiarity to anybody who has been involved in a similar process. But such experiences have seldom been committed to print, and Bud's paper is a valuable contribution to what must (if museums are to come of age) develop into a self-respecting critical historiography of exhibition and museum operation.

The second section includes three further papers, by Geoff Bowker on ambiguous representations of the sub-soil produced by the Schlumberger Company during the 1930s, by Lynch and Edgerton on representation in contemporary astronomy, and by Law and Whittaker on how technologies of representation are used by writers about acid rain research to represent that research to non-scientists.

The thrust of all three papers is to suggest, in the words of Bowker, that in these scientific forms of representation 'we have discovered a site of social conflict no less intense and fraught than we would find in an analysis of a tea room conversation in a university department' (p. 253).

The final section is taken up solely with a paper by Corrigan. Its title is 'Innocent stupidities: de-picturing (human) nature. On hopeful resistances and possible refusals: celebrating difference(s) – again' so we know exactly what we are in for, and we are not disappointed. Doubtless the (correct) response is that a doc (as [s]he ordered)-u-ment (did you? did I?) of this kind would have been the poorer without it; and perhaps so it would.

Overall, this is an interesting volume, with a good mixture of contributions which open up a number of significant areas, for museum workers as for others in the cultural field. It should help to stimulate fresh activity.

Picture Power: Visual Depiction and Social Relations, in: *Sociological Review*, Monograph 35, published by Routledge, 1988.

Taiwan: its natural history and its new natural science museum

FRANCIS Y.T. CHANG

National Museum of Natural Science, Taiwan

The island of Taiwan, which Westerners call Formosa, is a province of China, and also the largest island of the country. It lies roughly parallel to the south-eastern coastal line of the mainland of China and is separated from it by a channel of 130–220km wide. Shaped like a fish, the island is nearly 36,000 sq.km in area.

In 1949, after a civil war between the Communists and the Nationalist party, the national government of the republic of China moved to Taiwan to take a stand against the Chinese communists. The *status quo* has been maintained in the Taiwan strait ever since. All articulate bodies of opinion in China and Taiwan equally agree that Taiwan is today part of China; the bone of contention between the people's republic and the republic of China is which of them is the legitimate ruler of the two together. Because of this political division,

Plate 10   Front view of the National Museum of Natural Science, Taiwan, with Stage One building on the right and Stage Two building on the left. Photograph: courtesy National Museum of Natural Science, Taichung, Taiwan.

Taiwan occupies a special position in contemporary Chinese history distinguishing it from other provinces of China.

However, today classed in contemporary jargon as one of the 'newly-industrialized countries' of the Western Pacific, Taiwan has become a country as advanced as any in the world of comparable geographic and human dimensions. At the end of 1989 the population stood at 20 million (aborigines number about 332,000) with a per capita income of £4,000 and the trade surplus remains at £8,333 million, representing 12.5 per cent of GNP, the highest in the world.

The main topographic characteristic of Taiwan is the predominance of mountain system running from north to south for nearly the whole length. It separates the island into a mountainous district in the east and a plains district in the west. Plains below 100m occupy 31.3 per cent of the total surface of the island. Areas between 100 and 1,000m occupy 37.2 per cent and areas above 1,000m occupy 3.15 per cent.

Lying across the Tropic of Cancer, Taiwan provides habitat for tropical and warm temperate plants to survive at low levels from the south to north. With the greater part of the island covered by huge mountain ranges, tropical, temperate and alpine plants exist successively at different altitudinal ranges. The rugged topography further increases variation in the vegetation at all levels. Owing to the physiographical location, the favourable climate and plentiful moisture, the vegetation of Taiwan is extremely luxuriant. Over half of the total surface of the island is covered by a spectrum of six forest types, with a diverse flora of over 4,000 vascular plant species.

In his famous book *Island Life*, the Victorian Naturalist Alfred R. Wallace distinguished Taiwan as follows:

> It is crossed by the line of the Tropic Cancer a little south of its centre; and this position, combined with its lofty mountains, gives it an unusual variety of tropical and temperate climates. These circumstances are all highly favourable to the preservation and development of animals, from what we already know of its productions, it seems probable that few, if any, islands of approximately the same size and equally removed from a continent will be found to equal it in the number and variety of their higher animals (A.R. Wallace, *Island Life*, third edn (London 1905)).

Indeed, the unique physiographical situation of Taiwan supports a very rich fauna: 61 species of land mammals, 411 species of birds (156 resident species), 106 species of reptiles, 29 species of amphibians, 137 species of freshwater fish, about 15,000 insects species, including 400 species of butterfly and about 200 land snails are known to occur here.

Since 1970, due to the growing awareness of the unbalanced relationship with the natural environment in Taiwan – signified by heedless exploitation, appalling pollution, and disappearing species – the Taiwanese government has initiated a series of comprehensive conservation and educational programmes, among them, five national parks, eleven nature reserves and the National Museum of Natural Science.

In April 1981, the development office of the National Museum of Natural Science was established under the direction of the Ministry of Education. Based upon the ancient Chinese philosophy that the cosmos is a unified whole of heaven, earth and people, and the contemporary principles of ecological conservation, the museum's objective is to study and interpret the independence between nature and human beings. In accordance with this objective the museum has two missions. Firstly, to be a national centre for the study of Taiwain's natural history by collecting natural history objects and by making available to the science community the associated information. Secondly, to entertain and educate the public about the indivisible relationship between people and nature through displays and educational programmes (Plate 10).

To complete the above missions, the museum has devised four stages. Stage 1 consists of an auditorium and a science centre. The auditorium has a dome-shaped screen measuring 23m in diameter tilted at a 30° angle. Its main equipment includes a space-simulating system and an Omnimax film projection system. The average attendance rate is 85 per cent of the maximum capacity of 304. The science centre contains two exhibit halls, a science classroom, a discovery room, a computer room, a lecture hall and a video-tape corner. In total (including exhibition, education, public service and administration area) the stage 1 building covers 9,870 sq.m, and cost £9.3 million. This stage has been open to the public since 1986. The average attendance is 1.6 million per year or approximately 8 per cent of the population.

Stage 2 is the life science hall which consists of eight natural history galleries: origin of life, age of dinosaurs, the human story, the human body, food and population, sound in nature, colour in nature, numbers and forms, with a total exhibition area of 14,424 sq.m. Including the associated research departments and collection spaces,

Stage 2 covers an area of about 16,952 sq.m. The total cost was £19.5 million. Stage 2 has been opened to the public since august 1988 and has attracted nearly 1 million people per year.

The central theme of the Stage 3 is 'Chinese science and civilization'. It will include six galleries: science and inventions of China, Chinese agriculture, Chinese medicine, Chinese spiritual life, the story of the ancient Chinese and the culture of Taiwan aboriginals.

Stage 4, the last phase, will cover exhibitions on eight themes: the dynamic earth, the underground treasures, the mysterious sea, environment and human beings, conservation of species, matter and energy, the microscopic world and life on earth. In this stage, it will contain classroom/theatres, micrarium, dioramas, 3-D theatres and a bird's eye vision theatre to increase visitors' understanding of the earth and the current environmental issues.

Both Stages 3 and 4 are now under construction and scheduled to open in 1992. The total floor coverage wil be 56,393 sq.m, of which about 70 per cent will be the exhibition, education and public service area. It will cost approximately £36 million when complete.

The museum tries to make it clear that it is in the business of entertaining and educating people. Therefore, on the exhibition side, it includes the best available scientific and audio-visual materials, as well as exhibits with which visitors can interact in a variety of ways. On the education side, it involves activities which cover both the scientific and exhibition aspects. Being well aware that it is competing with other cultural and leisure attractions in Taiwan for visitors, the museum has to have a vigorous marketing programme which incudes:

(1)   A computerized booking system for visitors from different parts of the island to use;

(2)   A promotion centre in the Capital, Taipei, for advertising the museum (Taipei is in the north of Taiwan, this museum is in the centre.)

(3)   A monthly newsletter which is sent to every school in Taiwan, primary, junior, high schools and universities. In total about 3,000 copies.

(4)   Travelling exhibits and the provision of pre-visit or follow-up learning materials, to reach out to the country as a whole.

(5)   Regular liaison with science teachers to make sure the museum's educational programmes are tailored to the needs

of school groups, which account for 60 per cent of the visitors.

(6) The Environmental Education Research Unit, with the purpose of setting up a computer databank as a resource for schools, developing teaching materials and tools, and compiling illustrative cases on ecological education for teachers.

So much for the exhibit and educational programmes of the museum. Now, I would like to add a few words on the collecting and research function of the museum.

As mentioned above, the mission of the museum is to become the nationwide centre for the collection and research of Taiwan's natural history. Since it is a new museum, its collections and research work has to start from scratch. The collection policy is there but until now the museum only has approximately 100,000 specimens and artefacts. The museum will have a long way to go to achieve a comprehensive presentation of the island's rich flora and fauna either from taxonomic, geographical or historical coverage point of view. However, the Collection and Research Department of the museum now have eleven curatorial staff who are conducting research on local insects, amphibians, birds, microfossils, angiospermae, igneous rocks, minerals, material culture and ethnological art. The department has built geochemical, biological, botanical laboratories and a scanning electron microscope laboratory. To provide a precise references for the field investigations, it has also established a map centre. By the completion of stages 3 and 4 the department expects to have a staff membership of twenty-four, and the total collection and research space will exceed 25,000 sq.m, including a transmission electron microscope laboratory, an electron probe micro-analyser laboratory, an electrophresis laboratory and an X-ray laboratory.

Despite its fairly good exhibition galleries and various educational prorammes, the future prospect of the museum must be based on collections and scholarly research associated with those collections. We are well aware of the fact that collections are the *raison dêtre* of museum and the instrument of its educational role. It is to this aspect that I believe the National Museum of Natural science in Taiwan should devote most of its resources in order to be qualified as a first-rate natural history museum in the international museum community.

The crisis of representation in museums: the exhibition 'The Spirit Sings', Glenbow Museum, Calgary, Canada

GREG McMANUS

University of British Columbia Museum of Anthropology

The self-diagnosed 'crisis of representation' with which the discipline of anthropology is currently struggling has inevitably been extended to involve museums, in particular those which purport to represent 'others', and especially those in countries with indigenous populations. Questions such as 'Who should represent who?', 'How?' and 'By what authority?' have perhaps become largely theoretical problems for anthropology, but when asked of museums they provide serious challenges to the very existence and mandate of such institutions.

Increasingly, such challenges to museums are coming from the people being represented, the 'others' so to speak. This brief review intends to describe a recent instance of museum representation which came under challenge from the very people being represented, and which is likely to become a landmark in the history of the relationship between museums and indigenous peoples in the country concerned. The event referred to is the exhibition 'The Spirit Sings', organized by the Glenbow Museum in Calgary, Canada, to represent Native Canadian culture.

'The Spirit Sings' exhibition was organized as part of the Olympic Arts Festival, an event which ran alongside the 1988 Winter Olympic Games in Calgary, Alberta. The basic objective of the exhibition was to bring together, for the first time, the best examples of native Canadian material culture from collections around the world. Many of the objects selected had not been seen in Canada since their expatriation, in some cases more than three hundred years earlier.

For the purposes of the exhibition the native cultures of Canada were divided into six geographic regions based 'loosely on cultural and linguistic affiliations' (Harrison, 1987: 11). The research and curation of each culture area was the responsibility of a specialist in that area. It is important to note here that no members of the curatorial team were native Canadian. In fact, there was very little provision for native involvement in the exhibition process at any level. Although the curators were all fully paid for their work, a native consultation committee which was established operated on a purely voluntary basis which resulted in very few, if any, native people from outside Calgary becoming involved (Ames, 1989).

In short, 'The Spirit Sings' was a typically traditional ethnological exhibition in which a museum of the dominant culture attempted to represent the heritage of a minority culture, largely in its absence. This was not a departure from previously accepted practice in Canadian museums and in itself was not enough to make the exhibition controversial. However, 'The Spirit Sings' was sponsored by the giant petroleum company Shell Oil and this is when the Lubicon Lake Cree people entered the picture.

The Lubicon Lake Cree from northern Alberta have been engaged in a protracted and sometimes bitter land dispute with the Canadian and Albertan governments for over fifty years. Very briefly, it seems the Lubicon were overlooked by government agents searching for native groups to sign land treaties in the nineteenth century and have hence been without legal claim to reserve land ever since. Shell Oil entered the scene by leasing, alongside other oil and gas interests, huge tracts of the Lubicon claim from the Alberta government, reportedly at the rate of about $1.3 million a day (Myers, 1988: 12).

The Lubicon band announced in mid-April 1986 that it intended to call for a boycott of the 1988 Winter Olympics to draw attention to its unresolved land claims. Shortly afterwards their boycott call focused specifically on 'The Spirit Sings' exhibition. They justified their call in that the exhibition, which claimed to promote an understanding of native cultures and ultimately to benefit them, was being sponsored by Shell, one of the corporations working on land they claimed, and by the provincial and federal governments, which were not working towards a satisfactory settlement of their claim.

The Lubicon requested that museums around the world which had been asked to lend objects to 'The Spirit Sings' should not agree to loan. The Lubicon position was stated clearly in the letter sent by Lubicon Chief Bernard Ominayak to participating museums:

> We are organising this international boycott because the Calgary Winter Olympics are being sponsored by basically the same interests which are systematically trying to wipe us out as a people, so that they can steal our aboriginal lands and the valuable gas and oil resources which our aboriginal lands contain . . . . Display of these artifacts by the Glenbow . . .

could only serve to support efforts by these same interests to achieve enhanced international respectability and credibility (Ominayak, 1987: 1).

The Lubicon position found sympathy and support in many quarters. The news media was generally sympathetic to the native group and the boycott was actively supported by a number of native organizations in Canada and the United States. Academic anthropologists also came out overwhelmingly in support of the Lubicon.

In the museum world opinion was difficult to gauge. Very few Canadian museum professionals publicly voiced any opinion. Perhaps they saw peril in supporting either side lest they be seen to be either unsympathetic to native problems and aspirations or, on the other hand, unsupportive of their colleagues at the Glenbow. Foreign museums were less reticent. Several institutions withdrew from loan agreements with the Glenbow, some citing support for the Lubicon boycott call as the reason for doing so, others expressing concern for the safety of their objects considering the confrontational nature of the situation. In all, some 160 objects were withheld from the exhibition by foreign museums.

The Glenbow itself was unstinting in its position that the exhibition would not be 'held hostage' for political purposes by any group. There was seemingly never any question of 'The Spirit Sings' not going ahead, albeit without the objects withheld from loan. Despite the massive publicity campaign against it, the exhibition opened on time and ran its course. The only noticeable effect of the Lubicon action was the erection, at the request of several lending museums, of a notice at the end of the exhibition affirming support for a speedy and just resolution to native land claims and the related issues of compensation, self-determination, and self-government.

In all, some 650 objects were exhibited before a record 127,000 visitors to the Glenbow. However, no matter how successful 'The Spirit Sings' was as a museum exhibition, it will probably always be better remembered for the controversy that surrounded it and for the many issues which surfaced from that controversy. Much of the debate over the affair, especially that involving academic anthropologists and museum professionals, became more general than the specific Lubicon protest. The underlying issue, however, was simply that some of the people whose culture was 'on show' in the exhibition objected to their heritage being used, as they saw it, to benefit oil corporations and governments with which they have serious dispute.

In terms of 'the crisis of representation' mentioned at the beginning of this review, the Glenbow controversy has many implications for ethnological museums and for anthropology as a whole. Despite the general attitude within museums that their representations of 'others' must be objective and based on good scholarship, it is increasingly clear that no museum interpretation or representation can be objective or apolitical when it involves one group of people representing the culture of another.

This being the case, it should not have been such a surprise that the Lubicon people chose 'The Spirit Sings' as the target of their protests, despite the Glenbow's argument that a museum exhibition should *not* be a target for political action. As Halpin (1988: 92) notes in her review of the exhibition, the relationship between museums and native people in Canada has traditionally been an 'us and them' situation, with very few native people being involved in museum representations of themselves and their cultural heritage (Ames, 1989). 'The Spirit Sings' was an exhibition *about* native cultures, but was not an exhibition *by* or *for* native peoples, and this leads to the conclusion that it was perhaps an appropriate target for the Lubicon protest. If we accept, as I believe we must, that museum interpretation and representation is generally not a value-free, objective, or apolitical exercise, museums must be prepared to face and accept such challenges from the people whose lives and history are being interpreted and represented.

More importantly, contemporary museums must respond to such challenges and work towards resolving the 'crisis of representation' which, after all, could be interpreted as simply meaning that museums no longer have an inalienable right to deal with other peoples' cultural heritage without consultation, even as a minimum requirement.

One significant legacy of 'The Spirit Sings' affair is the resolution regarding the ethical aspects of exhibiting objects belonging to minority groups adopted by ICOM (the International Council of Museums). Proposed by the International Committee of Ethnological Museums as a direct response to the Lubicon – Glenbow controversy, the resolution reads:

Museums which are engaged in activities relating to living ethnic groups should, whenever possible, consult with the appropriate members of those groups, and such museums should avoid using ethnic materials in any way which might be detrimental and/or offensive to such groups (ICME, 1987).

Clearly then, the 'crisis of representation' is not simply a theoretical crisis for museums, especially those dealing with the cultural heritage of 'others'. As the Canadian example cited above illustrates, such museums are no longer immune from challenge, if they ever were, especially as indigenous peoples in countries such as New Zealand, the United States and Australia, as well as Canada, gain strength both politically and culturally. If the challenges are accepted, as I believe they must, and new relationships are forged, museums in these countries may well develop in unique, increasingly democratic, and very exciting directions.

Bibliography

Ames, M.M., Personal communication (November, 1989).
Halpin, M., Museum Review: 'The Spirit Sings', *Culture* 8 (1) a1988: 89–93.
Harrison, J.D., Introduction, *The Spirit Sings: Artistic Traditions of Canada's First Peoples* (McLelland and Stewart: Toronto, 1987): 10–16.
ICME, *ICME Newsletter No. 10*, International Committee of Museum Ethnology, 1987.
Myers, M., 'The Glenbow Affair', *Inuit Art Quarterly* 3 (1) 1988: 12–16.
Ominayak, B., Unpublished letter to M. Ames, University of British Columbia Museum of Anthropology, 18 February 1987.

The GREM conference, Montreal, Canada, 31 October–2 November 1990

JUDY HANLINE
Taranaki Museum, New Zealand.

GREM, which is an acronym for 'Le Groupe de recherche sur l'education et les musées' (Université de Québec), regularly hosts a biennial museum education conference. Conference proceedings are published and provide a valuable contribution to the growing material relating to museum education research and information.

The theme for the conference was 'A propos des approches didactiques du musée'. The conference was arranged and organized by Professor Michel Allard from the Département des Sciences de l'Education, together with a highly efficient and dedicated team of post-graduate students. The conference attracted approximately 240 participants. Conference delegates were representative of the many diverse groups interested in the expanding field of museum education – teachers, university lecturers and students, and museum professionals including curators, administrators, educators and directors. Participants were an exciting amalgam (museums of almost every genre were represented) of highly motivated people who obviously appreciate and value the all-encompassing role of education within the museum arena.

The conference theme established a number of concepts in relation to museum education. Participants were encouraged to analyse the various teaching approaches available in the museum, and to examine the functions of subject/object/agent. 'Subject' was understood as the person or group for whom the teaching/learning situation is set in place. 'Object' included the objectives and the context of the planned experience, which encompasses museum artefacts, exhibitions and so on, within the educative programmes of the particular museum. Objectives can be cognitive, affective or psychomoter. 'Agent' referred to the combination of human and material resources utilized in the teaching/learning situation, taking into consideration means/ strategies/experience/understanding.

During the morning session of the first day of the conference, Professor Michel Allard (Directeur du Groupe de Recherche sur l'Education et les Musées) outlined the background to GREM and gave a brief résumé of the research initiated and undertaken. This was followed by an address from Laurier Lacroix (Directeur, Maitrise en Museologie, Université du Quebéc à Montréal), and Suzanne Boucher (agente de recherche, GREM) presented a précis of the aims and objectives of the conference theme.

The afternoon of day one was devoted to a 'Table Ronde', an invigorating group comprising five guest speakers. Those presenting papers were Marcel Brisebois (directeur general, Musée d'Art Contemporain de Montréal), Jean-Pierre Cordier (Ingenieur d'Etudes, Conseil National de la Recherche Scientifique, Université de Paris V), Eilean Hooper-Greenhill (lecturer, Department of Museum Studies, University of Leicester, England), Helene Lamarche (Chef des

Services Educatifs, Musée des Beaux-arts de Montréal), and Judy Hanline (Education Officer, Taranaki Museum, New Zealand).

The Round Table was aimed at all conference participants in order to allow delegates: (1) to gain different perspectives relating to museum education; (2) to provide the opportunity to recognise different points of view; (3) to acknowledge these and examine their own perceptionsof museum education. These objectives were highly successful as was evidenced by the animated and frequently very forthright discussion which emanated from the floor during the extensive question and discussion period which followed the conclusion of the Round Table session. The allocation of a considerable time frame for discussion was a sound move by the conference organizers and allowed for valuable discourse between guest speakers and delgates.

The second and third days of the conference were dedicated to the following themes: the role of the agent in museum teaching and learning approaches with regard to the age of the visitors, and teaching approaches according to the type of museum and the museum collections.

The design of each half day's timetable contributed to the general conference theme. To add variety and spontaneity to the conference programme a series of workshops (some activity based) was organized which allowed frequent discussion between workshop leaders and participants. Each workshop had a leader, chairperson and recorder, and participants were able to select the workshop which covered their particular professional interests. The conference closed with an informal meeting. The aim of this particular assembly was to encourage an exchange of philosophy and ideas and to enable participants to reflect on the proceedings of the past three days.

GREM Conference was a highly successful museum education conference. The success was due to a number of factors. Firstly, a well chosen conference title and theme, which encapsulated many of the questions being raised by museum professionals. These questions are not only being raised in Québec but are being discussed world-wide by those concerned with all aspects of museum education. Secondly, the conference organization and programme planning was superb, an excellent mix of passive and active learning! Thirdly the invited speakers were an interesting and stimulating mix of museum professionals, and museum education academics – an admix which contributed to a balanced overview of museum education.

Call for papers for forthcoming volumes

The topic chosen for *New Research in Museum Studies* volume 3 is *Museums and Europe 1992*, and that for volume 4 is *Museums and the Appropriation of Culture*. These volumes will concentrate upon the chosen topics, but may also include papers which deal with other aspects of museum studies. The editor would be pleased to hear from any worker in the field who may have a contribution. Any ideas for papers or completed papers for consideration should be sent to Dr Susan Pearce, Department of Museum Studies, 105 Princess Road East, Leicester LE1 7LG.

Contributions to the reviews section, including reviews of conferences and seminars, videos, exhibitions and books, or any other museum event, are similarly welcomed, and should be sent to Dr Eilean Hooper-Greenhill at the above address.

Editorial policy

New Research in Museum Studies is a referreed publication and all papers offered to it for inclusion are submitted to members of the editorial committee and/or to other people for comment. Papers sent for consideration should be between 3,000 and 10,000 words in length, and may be illustrated by half-tones or line drawings, or both. Prospective contributors are advised to acquire a copy of the *Notes for Contributors*, available from the editor, at an early stage.

New Research in Museum Studies has a policy of encouraging the use of non-sexist language, but the final decisions about the use of pronouns and so on will be left to individual authors. However, the abbreviation s/he is not to be used.

The editor wishes it to be understood that she is not responsible for any statements or opinions expressed in this volume.

Notes on contributors

Susan M. Pearce read history at Somerville College, Oxford, and remained at Oxford for postgraduate work in archaeology. She gained her PhD from Southampton University in 1981. She had curatorial posts at the National Museums on Merseyside and Exeter City Museum, was appointed Senior Lecturer in Museum Studies in the Department of Museum Studies, University of Leicester in 1984, and took over as Director of the Department in 1989. She is interested in the interpretation of material culture and the meanings of objects, and the history and nature of museum collections. This has drawn her to Bronze Age studies (the subject of her doctoral thesis and Somerville College Fellowship Grant, 1984) and Inuit material (research work in Arctic, Churchill Fellowship, 1974). She has published a wide range of papers and eight books, including *The Bronze Age Metalwork of South Western Britain, Museum Studies in Material Culture* (edited) and *Archaeological Curatorship*. She edits the book series *Leicester Museum Studies*. She was a visiting lecturer at Berkeley University, California in 1982, and lectures widely.

Eilean Hooper-Greenhill trained as a sculptor at the University of Reading followed by several years teaching in a large London comprehensive school. A five-year period of varied freelance art teaching projects in museums, galleries, schools, colleges and art centres in London and the South East, preceded an appointment in the Education Department at the National Portrait Gallery. Since 1980, Dr Hooper-Greenhill has been lecturing in the Department of Museum Studies, University's of Leicester. Dr Hooper-Greenhill's MA thesis researched the National Portrait Gallery as an agent of cultural reproduction, using some of the educational and cultural theories of Basil Bernstein. Her PhD was awarded from the University of London in 1988, and used the theories of Michel Foucault to re-read museum histories. Dr Hooper-Greenhill has published extensively on museums and their social role. She is the author of *Museums and Gallery Education*. Dr Hooper-Greenhill is a Trustee of the Horniman Public Museum and Public Park Trust and the mother of two children.

Dr Peter Johnson is a Reader in Economics at the University of Durham. He previously held posts at the University of Nottingham and at University College, Cardiff. His main research interests are in applied economics. In the last few years he has specialized in the analysis of new firm formation and in the employment effects of tourism. He has recently co-directed (with Dr Barry Thomas) a major project, financed by the Joseph Rowntree Foundation, on the local economic impact of the North of England Open Air Museum, Beamish. He has worked as a consultant for a number of public agencies.

Dr Barry Thomas is a Senior Lecturer in Economics at the University of Durham. He has held lecturing/research posts at the Universities of Salford, Liverpool and Warwick. His principal research interests have been in labour markets and the evaluation of public policy, and more recently in the economics of tourism – especially its employment effects. He has also undertaken research into economic aspects of museums. He has worked as a consultant for several government bodies.

Peter Jackson BA, PhD, FRSA, Professor of Economics and Director of the Public Sector Economics Research Centre, University of Leicester since 1977; previously employed as an Economic Adviser to HM Treasury 1969/71 and as lecturer in economics at Stirling University. Chair of the Council for National Academic Awards Social Sciences Committee and a member of the Board of the Public Finance Foundation. Author of *Public Sector Economics* (fourth edn 1990 jointly with C.V. Brown) and the *Political Economy of Bureaucracy* (1982). Professor Jackson has recently published (with D.R. Palmer) *First Steps in Performance Measurement* which reports some of the material of a research project financed by the Leverhulme Trust. Professor Jackson has published widely on the subject of public expenditure analysis and public sector management and is currently joint editor of the journal *Public Money and Management*.

Nich Pearson is the author of *The State and the Visual Arts* (Open University Press, 1982), *Art Galleries and Exhibition Spaces in Wales* (Welsh Arts Council, 1981) and articles on art, artists and the economics of the arts. Has worked for the Welsh Arts Council as Visual Art Marketing Officer, and taught at Newport College of Art and Leicester University. Co-researched and co-authored the Gulbenkian report on *The Economic Situation of the Visual Artist*. Currently employed as Senior Policy and Development Officer with the Welsh Consumer Council. Special interests include William Morris' development of a Marxist analysis of art (contributions to catalogue to ICA 1984, 150th anniversary Morris exhibition and to William Morris Society *Journal*).

Guy Wilson MA, FSA has been Master of the Armouries since 1988. He is Director of the National Museum of Arts and Armour at HM Tower of London and a national expert and international adviser on the subject. His duties include presentation, custody and display of the collection at the Tower and other historic monuments and museums in the UK and overseas. Educated at Oxford and Manchester Universities, he joined the Royal Armouries in 1972, was appointed Keeper of Edged Weapons in 1978 and Deputy Master in 1981. Mr Wilson is a member of the British Commission for Military History, the Advisory Committee on Historic Wreck Sites, Arms and Armour Society of Great Britain and Denmark, and the Meyrick Society. He has written extensively on the subject of arms and armour including: *Treasures from the Tower, Treasures of the Tower: Crossbows*, and articles for *Connoisseur, Guns Review, The Burlington, The Journal of the Arms and Armour Society of Great Britain*, and other specialist journals and magazines. He is currently working on a translation of Josef Alm's classic work *A Survey of the European Crossbow*, editing and revising it from a Swedish translation to produce the first English translation of this work.

The post of Master of the Armouries dates back to the Middle Ages when the title would have translated as 'Keeper of the Royal Wardrobe' since it involved care of kings' accoutrements and weapons. He is the eighteenth person to hold the actual title 'Master'. A famous past Master was Queen's Champion and tournament organizer to Queen Elizabeth I, Sir Henry Lee, whose armour is on show at the Tower. Guy Wilson is married with four children.

Patricia E. Kell is currently working towards a PhD in Museum Studies at the University of Leicester, focusing on learning behaviour at historic sites. She was previously educated at the University of Toronto, where she gained a BSc and a master's degree in Museum Studies, and at the Université de Montreal, where she obtained an

MSc in anthropology. She has worked primarily for the Canadian Parks Service both at the site level as an interpreter and at the regional and national levels doing interpretation-based research.

William Chapman teaches historic preservation (conservation) in the School of Environmental Design, the University of Georgia in Athens, Georgia, USA. Previously he has held positions in the Division for Archaeology and Historic Preservation for the US territory of the Virgin Islands and has worked as an administrator for cultural programmes in the US National Park Service. His special areas of research are Caribbean cultural history, particularly the vernacular architecture of the region, building conservation, and conservation planning. He holds a DPhil in Anthropology from Oxford University and an MSc in historic preservation from the School of Architecture, Planning and Historic Preservation at Columbia University in New York. He has published extensively on conservation and the history of archaeology and historic preservation, including a recent article in the *Antiquaries Journal* on British archaeologists in the 1860s. He is currently working on a book-length study of the nineteenth-century archaeologist Augustus Pitt Rivers and his contributions to anthropology and antiquities protection.

Charles Hunt graduated in Anthropology from University College, London University in 1964. He has since worked in a number of museums, including as Assistant Keeper in the Department of Ethnography of the British Museum, Keeper of Ethnology in Liverpool Museums (National Museums on Merseyside), and Director of the Fiji Museum. He is currently curator of the Anthropological Museum of the University of Aberdeen. His main interests are in Oceanic art and archaeology, and the history and philosophy of museums.

Index